Demon Commuter

and other poems

Some advance praise for *Demon Commuter:*

Poet Steve Hirsch demonstrates in this fine collection that he is dialed into the Yin Yang and is rocksolid in his perceptive faculties. *DEMON COMMUTER* gives us finely tuned poems, paeans of praise and terse phillipics that halt and haunt the reader, alter the consciousness, long after reading. Hirsch asks the big questions, and he asks them memorably: How do you stay alive when each heartbreak saps your life away? How do you keep the story straight when half the world is crooked? No mere collection of rant or woke rap, these poems hit their mark time again with rapier-like exactitude, draw blood, and bound irrepressibly along to their next target, often reaching incantatory power as they go. *DEMON COMMUTER* transforms astute reportage into a rare and penetrating running commentary. This is fine poetry, poetry. that weaves spun magic with poise and aplomb. Hirsch gives the current and the topical the quasi-mythical aura it deserves.

— George Wallace, writer in residence, Walt Whitman Birthplace

Steve Hirsch's readers expect a lot: great poems of corralled consciousness barely contained in words stretched to the breaking point. Hirsch captures the unique moment, but his imagistic precision mingles intimately with the recognition of the socio-political-historical dimension of the scenes of his life, and with a view longer yet, his lines are lit with glints of what does not change, the illumination which is for him less a conviction than a habit of vision, nothing more than the way things look.

In its most literal reading the title refers to Hirsch's (and many other workers') daily routine, the commute to earn a living, the mental "drivenness" imposed by the reality principle. Taking a step back, Hirsch makes it clear that his own sometimes ill-fitting vocation is embedded in an inescapable system that privileges greed and aggression, giving the demonic the face of war and exploitation. Yet in his final vision, everything is transformed, redeemed even, and "demon" can regain a numinous glow. But even once the demon of the title has appeared in beneficent form as the sort of interior muse of which Socrates spoke, now and then he seems more closely to resemble S. Clay Wilson's Checkered Demon in his frantic, barely controllable impulsive energy.

— William Seaton, author of *Spoor of Desire* and *Planetary Motions*

In "a world networked by things yet bereft of insight," *Demon Commuter*'s achievement is in its volatile and contradictory enmeshment. At once a political and social commentary that harkens back to his lineage studies with Allen Ginsberg, Steve Hirsch's poetry speaks with "a prescient vertigo" to these times. I'm struck by this collection's descriptive and theatrical power, staged from deep within the infotech gig economy where workers are laid low like swine and maligned bosses flourish. While others might see this work as one of pervasive Kaliyuga darkness and despair, I wholeheartedly agree with the author that "This poetry is a rescue from the death of all dreams."

— Jim Cohn, author of *Treasures for Heaven*

The violence of these poems is a mode of anguish. We are at the crossroads, the place where the only possible action may (or may not) occur, "our faces marked by sleep and by the surface of dream rivers that sparkle with purpose"; "the day," the narrator says, "is a drug that causes amnesia / and night disguises dreams we can't maintain or remember." One imagines these poems being written as the poet moves, still half-drugged with sleep. from home to office, then from office to home. "Crushed leaves trail demarks another year in mulch strata." The purity of the attack extracts its necessary payment, yet he goes on with an amazing narrative that asserts the speaker's place amid and apart from the horrors he documents with such eloquence. It is all a nightmare, to be sure, but it is a nightmare in which language moves straight out of Ginsberg City into the astonishing Trumpery of our time. If "Howl" was the cry of bohemian youth, this book is the cry of corporate middle age, but in both cases we get "the full hit of the 'truth,'" "the death inside of all":

Their voices won't leave me alone
but I am too far gone; way way beyond...

With grand eloquence and linguistic brio, Demon Commuter tells us all to awaken: "Home is always over there."

— Jack Foley, host and executive producer of "Cover to Cover with Jack Foley"

Demon Commuter

and other poems

Steven L. Hirsch

Giant Steps Press

www.GiantStepsPress.com

The author would like to acknowledge the following publications in which many of the poems in this volume first appeared: *Napalm Health Spa Report, Hunger, In/Filtration, CAPS Annual, Big Scream, The Long Islander, Walt's Corner*, and *Poetrybay.*

The author is deeply grateful to the following people who gave their time to help this book be published in its best form: Kirpal Gordon, Karen Hirsch, and Jacqueline Ahl. Many thanks as well to Darrell Johnsson, Pavla Johnssonova, and all my teachers and collaborators over the years.

Hirsch, Steven L., 1960 –

Demon Commuter

ISBN: 978-1-958266-03-8

Printed in The United States of America.
Cover design by Steve Hirsch © 2023
Back cover author photo by © Karen Hirsch

First Edition
GIANT STEPS PRESS
GiantStepsPress.com

This book is dedicated to all those who commute to a city for a living

Table of Contents

Friends of The People

Ugly World, Beautiful Planet

Bright spring sun through young leaves.
Putin smirks on his non-victory day
while babies die by genocide in Ukraine.

At the terminal, the fact that we are all terminal
sends the masked crowd shuffling into the bowels of the subway.
Placard with no numbers; filament of signal dims
the bud electric and accelerant
caretaker fumbler blindered by the simulation.

Things fade away vividly
with clear and painful delivery
a smudge of grease on the glass.
In my grunting and grief
the light makes it through
like blood through a sieve.

Strong wind surprise almost
picks you up
into the shadow dance
into Jasmine and dried bouquet —
Smell horror on the precipice of lemon sorbet;
nineteen more children murdered at school by a damaged schoolmate.

Drink, sweet Jasmine
climb the draperies for fun.
Brief life such a hard thing to swallow.
Inhale pollen, honey shards and cinnamon
stirred by new dragonflies and hummingbirds.
Black butterfly lands and a child dies.
Young doe munches new grass up the mountainside.
Pyramids above the Kremlin and Pentagon; pilots & govts see them
but no one will help us.
We are under attack from ourselves, the alien within.

Bullets burrow into the hill with fast mechanisms of escape.
Soft wood and bone bends; trees and bodies crack and fall
small circles of red emerge and spread.
Parents reach to touch today's wall of photos
as funerals wail and weep down the street.

Chant an angry dirge at deaf politicians
unable to feel, accept risk, change beliefs.

Dead Jasmine; crisp white flowers fall on my desk.
Every CNN report hurts, a long list of the lost
lands hard.
Breaking news; deja vu, damage is done to you too.

Long Harley ride with Jesse over cool sunny roads to Roscoe.
Blanketed horses chew the landscape.
Sky so blue it looks fake.
News so bizarre it must be too.

Friends of The People

Where do shallow imperatives end and real intentions begin?
Where is the line?
The bigger the lie
the more these voices rescind tolerance.

Brianna's sweet heart and caring eyes cancel the canceler;
she rolls the tape to show the red-handed crime denied.
Jake refuses to take the Blue pill or the Red.
Poppy pierces the dead-pan panderer's blank gaze.
Ari disabuses the sham testimony of a liar unfazed.

Everyone wants reparations
for being born.
How do you stay alive
when each heartbreak saps your life away?
How do you keep the story straight
when half the world is crooked?

Wolf rocks the situation room with gravel & gravity.
Fareed spills the secrets of the state, exact position
of a country divided, shines a light on hate
the imperfect union hidden beyond bias.

The stupid will ignore; deniers will deny.
You can hate the haters all day and still you're a hater.
If you don't know by now how many sides to a coin
you'll never win another election again.
White people dwindle while swindlers swindle
stash their stolen cash in crypto.

Avlon sings a song of reality check with the morning birds.
Kate holds her ground in quicksand and dances en pointe.
Acosta cuts off congressmen who cower from compassion.
Bash does just that with a hammer forged in facts
bright knives to blind election deniers with haunting regret.

The inside is more important than the outside.
We come and go and go nowhere
in futile ping pong castigation of the other.
Afghanistan, Iraq, N. Korea, Iran, Russia —
Wounds of earth and man unbound and bloody.

The game is no game and no one is winning.
Andrea angers assholes with persistent questions they won't answer.
Rachel regards truth as god, law, and salvation and never wavers.
Brian beats the drum of accountability, silver-tongued and dumbfounded.
Brooke bags the basket case that broke the rules and releases the hounds.
Ministers of disruption attach fixtures of hope to your doorframe instead of blood.

Senior kills senior; child kills child; shooter kills a dozen
        and then himself, always a him —
Everything is a double-edged sword, dorje thrown to kill Mahakala.
Get smart — I could be your voice but I won't hold my tongue.
I won't let anything slide; the clock ticks on Democracy —
"If anything can be faked then anything can be denied."

Chalian chuckles as fools bark up dead desert trees with deadly weapons cocked.
Costello's class shines through the glare with hair's breath vision klaxon ablaze.
Pamela parades pedophiles in walk of shame sexting ku klux cataclysm.
Bianna, the piercing, pretty pied piper of genuine outrage at mind-prison's wardens.
Joy busts a move, a myth, and all bubbles of fraud
smug racist grin falls to grimace in the sharp light of articulate intelligence.

Don't get into a stare-down with David and Pierre 'cause you'll lose in despair.
No-nonsense Norah knows how information and money flow down corridors of power.
Superhero Psaki eats Fox reporters like cheeseballs and comes out smelling like flowers.
Bad governors tremble at the mere mention of Fox on the Hill sniffing controversy.
Gergen gargles blood of partisan gargoyles with calm, composed apotheosis.
Zeleny zooms in on the threat from within and makes it clear the North will rise again.

Marvelous Maher foresaw the coup, makes fun of the most sacred delusions and
sparks one up.
Sanjay sports caduceus tie, saves more lives than a hundred guns could snuff.
Ana's eyes define the high-minded regard for the ideas that clarify confusions.
Engel is kissed by Ukranian momma for being here and being there at once.
Cupp delivers a steaming pile of nails to the silent carpenters of common sense.
Fredricka defrocks frauds and files reports that show what's real and what's illusion.
Erin erases doubt that justice will prevail at long last like a lotus in mud.

This wild orgy of wit & wisdom with some of the smartest and most beautiful
people on earth!
Journalists ripped with washboard stomachs of mirrored steel!
Chain me to them for eternity! Make me their palm fan!
Without their sage oracle, any republic would fail.
They are the living contraception to the birth of falsehood!

Clarissa in a burka at Kabul Airport showing U.S. folly to the world
as desperate Afghan falls to death from the landing gear of a departing C-17.
Flags soaked in blood weakly lift and drip in 110 degree sand-oven breeze.
Hell's convection cracks the skin and spirit as babies are thrown over barbed wire.
The president flees reason and the scene as it devolves into endless funeral pyres.

Primitive Taliban lizard-brain so afraid of a smart and beautiful woman!
Confederate liars ply darker and wider veils over the eyes of the divine feminine!
Read – scan – cast - drop every report like a dime on delusion!

O, the humanity!
The heartless slaughter of innocent men, women and children by
the real enemy of the people and all who rally behind him!
May he face each and every one of them in judgment!
His hooves tap in fear on gold-rimmed marble as the camera pans an arc around him.
His fangs drip with blood, only discord emanates from him.

Tic Tok - Tic Tok - Hard Times - End Times - Extraordinary Times - whatever doom —
Time is passing fast like painting a flower without a stem
that becomes a symbol of itself — arising from nothing.
Petals fall into space to return there again
running out of a bottomless hourglass.

Future reports:

American Taliban wage war on women — This is how the south is lost.
Supreme Court allows slavery to return — A mass exodus from Texas.
Move the wall up a state and let them weave bullwhips, make stone clubs
paint barn hexes.
Daughter of an important liar loses his heir and her life by hand of law.
This is the cost of religious stupidity, deep-brain primitive flaw.

Elohim descend over the capitol in a red cloud
bring new tablets to command our kind;
deliver those that cannot live as one with all
in reverse rapture to another cloudy place where all is toil
and everyone is blind.

The irrelevant angle of a dull blade cannot cut the nut or part curtains.
Tucker, Trey, Sean, Laura, Jeanine, Steve, Ainsley, Brian
shuffle fantasies to let the empty caucus stay focused
on phantom facts and alternative realities they themselves
wouldn't want part of.

Be my friend and tell the piecemeal populace that populism won't protect them!
Be my friend and get the vaccine or breathe your last breath on a lung machine!
Be my friend again and again morning noon and night on every screen!
Be my friend god damn it and stop telling lies you sons of bitches!

Be my friend before the world ends.

4 Phone Calls with Putin

The Moscow visitor condo patrol
gathers dirty laundry and bad advice
"...take her to bed and wake in wet sheets...
...take her out to the shed and regret it."
Secretly take Putin's phone call
a tutorial on how to stage a coup in 4 years time by the "big lie" method
satisfy his $450 million in debt
with blame reversal.

Curses follow revolution.
Insurrection follows a fool.
Seems like an easy plan
just maintain the delusion at all costs.
"Don't call me friend and I'll call you a cause of global trouble.
Novachuk is not a river in Siberia so don't cross me."

"You must never, ever, give up the lie.
You must turn their weapons into feathers.
You must gather dirt on everyone, insult everyone.
You must segment and retaliate."

"Keep the count going; don't stop counting.
Keep fostering doubt instead of Guatemalans.
Keep the call loud and couched in free speech.
Keep the threat level high and facts out of reach.

Turn everything around and blame the other.
Turn against anyone that opposes you and make it personal.
Turn brother against brother, father against son.
Turn away from the love you were shown by your mother.

Put troops on every border.
Build walls to isolate people in the name of protecting them.
Shame those with integrity and call them weak.
Tag your opponents with doubt every time you speak.

Finally, my friend, when you start to feel shame
double down and start again.
Stand up and shout with insistence and fire
that wrong is right and orange is the new white."

Armed with what-about-isms and a horizon of misery
Vlad the scum-paler, smirched by the initial transcription — "Nyet nyet
History will only remember the winners in spite of the lies."
burns the transcriber's notes in the *'krugovoy'* file.

Krugovoy= "circular"

Crazy Fucking Shit

Cases drop; cases flip open, basket cases, secret antidote cases
a nuclear football, a bold lie told ten times, the passive message is to die.

Let's take a look at this madness, at the racist faces
let's take a good hard look at the crazy fucking shit that is going down.

Mental cases of the Trump base
in flagrant abasement of our shared presumption of safety.
Pace yourself; the reaper is just getting started, sharpening his blade
his flared nostrils rape the air.

One word filters through the dark mist and announces itself: Truth.
Truth is here, largely ignored.
The word passes into the hollow space of absence.

Breathe into it. Lean into it. Get used to it. Truth.
Breath into Black Lives Matter, our national fragility critical —
We race to awakening
not wokeness and not in theory.
Lean into the painful legacy: Ruthless slave-masters cracking bullwhips
across the backs of a chain gang; 10 million hypocritical blind eyes turned up north
so cloth can roll off the binary loom.

Cases rise; cases get hoses shoved down their throats, cases expire —
Breathe into absence.

Case of a government failing; a huge failure.
One million dead to date shake ghostly blue fists.

Case in point: "Person–Woman–Man–Camera–TV".
Case proves he is not sane; insane in every way, very scary.

Cases of Goya beans and Hydroxychloroquine stacked in rows around the Oval Office.
The resolute desk reeks with supremely white 'burder'-fart fascism.

Cases rise higher; coffins fall closed, hopeless cases, 2 months on a vent cases —
The heartache; golden calf incitement to riot around the idol, grab a pussy, cause a fight.

Willing to accept one percent of our children dying in a rush back to class.
Willing to allow a red-ass fascist oligarch to transform our fragile democracy into
New Russia.

Willing to hang at a local tap, elbow to elbow with tars and wanderers.
Willing to run our shuddering machines with the blood of our parents and grandparents.
Willing to hand the arsonist a torch and gas can.
Crazy fucking shit — all of it man.

Willing to say "It is what it is" about one million dead.
Willing to brag and deflect, skirt the surface without introspection, lie again and again
unable to feel and understand anything but what props up his heavy head.
So full of anger, greed, and fear; Pied Piper of the deranged right
leads his dumb flock off a cliff into an active volcano.
Willing to destroy the Post Office and advise his base to drink Drano
to rid themselves of the deadly virus he claimed was a hoax but knew better.

Evil mental case with his finger on the button of herd mentality.
Tweets from the golden toilet soil the media-stream.
He leaps from lie to lie like stone to stone across a raging river
as a party drowns and burns, flushed down by a rush to stupidity.
Volley of nuclear options never consider the people taking the real hit.
Crazy fucking shit, all of it.

President super-spreader death-wish hypocrite.
Crazy Fucking Shit!
Ego monster calling everyone a monster, demanding alms for the rich and stupid.
Crazy Fucking Shit!

He salutes an empty lawn, gasps for breath, sharpens his final claw.
Not even two weeks infected and he declares himself cured
with an experimental treatment no one can afford.
Even allies are enemies in his twisted brown-shirt
power-mad Nazi-grab toward the past.

Stand by stupid boys and proud of it.
Stand by as the world burns and towns drop into sink holes
and floods destroy our food sources.
Stand by true and Blue, ready to make a stand against science-denying, alt-right misfits
all crazy fucking pig-shit that wallow in their sty
a place where all you miscreants that said 'let's just give him a chance!'
should be confined to whine and ask
'why should we be stained with the mud we've flung?'
'why should we care if people die?'

2018 Overcast Forecast Recap

Though there are some shreds of blue
among the white clouds, a red pall
descends, the echo of a revisited forecast.
The country, and all of us peasants present
struggle under the idiot thumb of a giant orange ogre
from a fairytale nightmare.

Our government is being held hostage by a jealous god
a hungry ghost whose thirst for power is at odds
with the greater good and public will.
Dark base smug and righteous supreme white god at odds with truth.
Original sin wears the mask of a lizard-brain swamp-monster terrorist.
Whether our country or our species survives lies in the hands of a con man.

Life is the big cheat that always leaves you incomplete
just as late winter sun is cast across the trees under Orion's belt
that glows as night grows and makes it hard to see
the forest for the stellar trees, our ancestries mirrored
as above so below; it's quite a feat.

Cheek roughened, knee skinned, ego torn on the E train at 7th & 53rd
about as much fun as riding the bus after a prostate biopsy.
Port Authority escalator rattles up to the 5:20.
Bus to Central Valley rattles up a
ramp to the quickway bumper chain.
Electric seat and wheel warms the frozen whittling rattle-wince
as I crawl crumbled county roads home in disrepair.

Blood Wolf Moon eclipse takes on the weight of an omen
or a call to howl and find your pack or set your traps
to ensure next year there'll be another recap.

We ask the masters:
Does the path lead us where it wills
or do we take the path where we will?
Do we know where it leads
and why do we need to walk a path at all?
The sky and seasons tell us to drive forward in the direction
we're pulled anyway, the way we intend
to face the daily detours, obstacles and pitfalls

shell of a philosophical dilemma denied
as everyone around you slowly dies incomplete —
Mind is quite effete in the face of it.

Taught what we don't want, ask the next blue hope
to reflect the face of America and all at once
reverse the betrayal, chase the foxes from their henhouse.
Meanwhile the tumor grows and the cancer spreads.
No room for another hand in the cookie jar
to reap the dividends and tax refunds.

Cage shaken, apocalypse in progress, war to maintain sanity
war to prevent a wall, war to walk free as a minority in America
to be able to vote and live anywhere we please;
war to eradicate a deeply rooted disease
born of shame, fear, and delusion of supremacy.

Recap *is* the overcast forecast; more of the same in sight.
Hope hurts to hold in the heart, heavy and countered by fact.
Dark Age madness infected by cloak and cataract.
Broken heart aflame and harder to heft each year
like a backpack for the daily shlep torn and filled with holes
everything falling out and away onto the cold road.

My tax refund will go to wealthy US oligarchs whose only trickle down
is the drool that flies off their maw
as they laugh at getting more for themselves.
Deregulate the prison so the jailers can tighten their grip.
Let poison flow down sky, river, and stream so one day
we will need to buy our water and air in order to live and breathe.

Mueller says 'No Collusion' and the world seethes.
Politicians drop back into their pockets;
lobbyists order lobster and filet mignon
while I pick up a chicken and a box of Stove Top at Stop & Shop.
Recap is déja vu and I am caught in a Groundhog Day sign-on loop:
'Credentials unrecognized; please reenter or click *'forgot myself'*.'
'Account Locked after 3 unsuccessful attempts.'
'Impeachment denied; please try again.'

Pipebombs and Pressure Cookers

Children reduced to granules of explosive
in a pipebomb of peace via social media
to penetrate the US pressure cooker
building steam in America's twilight
like an old locomotive heading west
into setting sun behind puffs of black coal smoke.

The month's deathtoll of young lives climbs
yet all we hear are tweets about leaks, lies
and self-aggrandized postures —
        Silence from white-asshole-house and NRA.
Gun money exchanges hands
yet the social problems stand.
We rake the coals to get them hot
yet decry the burns that follow —
        Silence after ten more die at school.
        Silent thoughts and prayers, silent tears
        and silent pain — Loss suffered silently echoes.

Sickness from the top down
escalates within the base.
Backward policies season the braise
with fake/not-fake taste
mouths filled with nails.

Ryan, McConnell, and Sessions with mouth corners pulled down;
a chain-gang of heavy-joweled Silvio Dantes from the Sopranos.
They attack each other with big, incredulous, self-righteous puppy dog eyes;
murderous, complicit, shifty, hissing eyes.
Pressure cooker heads ready to burst with shit-for-brains pudding!

I'm tired of apples painted orange
hate mudras as badge of honor
torches, period.
I'm sick and tired of the phrase 'counter-intuitive'
when it really is just criminal.
So very tired of small thoughts tweeted by tiny minds on the toilet pre-dawn
proud to pinch a crap on the national stage.

Steam released through orange nostrils
sniffed back like Dennis Hopper in Blue Velvet.
With wild-eyed crazy ego-temper
he lobs another pipebomb across the aisle
clank clank-et-ee-clank clank.... hissssssssss — BLAM!

Let's have a summit; let's cancel the summit and light the big fuse.
Let's investigate the investigator; didn't Stalin try that ruse?
Let's rape the environment one more time for old time's sake.
Let's justify our duplicitous abuse and blame the past!
Let's make America Hate Again! Against the grain again! Rob the poor again!
Clank clank-et-ee-clank clank.... hissssssssss — BLAM!

Fill the swamp with rich men; give them the tax cuts.
Hand critical institutional control over to those exact counter-intuitives
to surely deconstruct, destabilize, debilitate and demonize every standard.
Drop a lie-bomb daily wherever you feel afraid and without a giant palm fan
to ease you back on your settee with a bunch of grapes.
Clank clank-et-ee-clank clank.... hissssssssss — BLAM!

Red-faced shame and admitted guilt pardoned by the guiltiest one of all
unable to side-step the obvious critical mass building to a taut squeak.
Pressure building to even the score, to tell the truth more; to show a single
shred of humility, humanity, even-handed justice stabbed through the hand
tipped scales heavy with history's repetition of failed fascist coups.
Clank clank-et-ee-clank clank.... hissssssssss — BLAM!

Farting on golf courses far and wide as he waddles from hole to hole
press pundits clamor for every gaff; every nod, every sniff, every piss-soaked smug smile
below his ghostly inverse raccoon eyes.
Bags punctuate the spray tan
and comb-over that looks like a stained rug.
Bite the bullet and lock n' load folks. The whole damn game is changed!
Congress on ice and a blue wave's-a-risin'; let's get back to the garden.
Clank clank-et-ee-clank clank.... hissssssssss — BLAM!

Update - Update — We have the House! — Investigate!
Update - Update — The coup of Justice has begun — Conflate, Congratulate!
Recapitulate and recalculate, clarify and objectify; appeal to the last thin shred
of sanity that remains.
BLAM! BLAM!
Blame the blamer until his shame irradiates and becomes permanent!
Incarcerate and penetrate the liars lies with the pride of an iron cage!

Celebrate and validate the fall of the swamp into itself; collude and collapse! Immolate, cremate and crack!

BLAM! BLAM! BLAM!
BLAM! BLAM! BLAM!
BLAM! BLAM! BLAM!

2019 Recap & Forecast from Hell

Antibiotic-resistant pigs chew their kin and shit pathogens.
Oh no the ribs smoke ring is a centimeter short!
I am eating my own arm and guts out all over the grill.
I am eating myself to death; trichinosis worm pores sweat
as I curate a war between Estée Lauder and Accenture.

Step into a bees nest at Warner Music Group.
Karmic payback for all those years as a Napster pirate.
My Vuze and my muse both corrupt my system.
I too am both a genius and a fool.
My boss wrote me up with HR because
I AM TURNING 60 AND SICK AND TIRED OF TAKING SHIT! That's why.
So he posted my job on *Indeed* to replace me.

I have faked it to make it most of my career.
Not formally trained in IT, I learned as I went.
Oh no a drama major with his hands on the network!?
I still can't see how software can be poetry though I try
and don't care if I'm a failure at those things, even if I rely
on this glass road to survive; ego purple with bruises, lies and left turns.
I've seen the underside of so many buses I could be an MCI mechanic.

We learned that up to thirty-seven percent of this amazing country
are actually bigoted white supremacists stuck in
a twisted past who lash out at minorities to compensate
for their own failure to deserve such a country
for their own low-brow, lizard-brain, cowardly fate.
A lie a minute, a crime an hour, the reins of power pulled tight
to bewitch the racially pure with messages of hate on the precipice of their flat earth —
OUTRAGE!

The impeachment of the devil leaves everyone with burning tongues, burning hands
and pants and hoarse throats, exhausted from hearing his name.
Now forever impeached, forever branded
a liar and a cheat, forked tongue, marginally sane
to claim Thomas Edison lives and the invention of the wheel.
Willing to steal anything he can, brazenly defiant loser
tweets with prehistoric venom against all accusers.

The Constitution in flames — Democracy on a pike.
A trial with no witnesses is a joke, hard to take.

The King of Kansas City, Kansas guilty of another rape.
Lady Liberty with her robes down around her ankles
gets the mushroom head of the devil, creates a baby fiefdom
that enslaves the common man to a dead-end future and new holocaust
where bloody revolution is the only way to decide which kingdom rules.

Disciplined animals climb subway stairs legs burning, puff steam into
face masks normalized against the scourge of COVID-19;
broke in so many ways and unable to change the game.
Scared to travel, emboldened bigots go more deeply insane.
No one is learning; no one cares about the future.
Get what you can while you can and to hell with everyone else.

We tried, we impeached, we marked the devil with his number.
We moved from Saturn to Mars, from delusion to democracy reclaimed.
We told the truth, paid our price, and we named names.
There's no looking back but we must get back.
There's no way of telling just from the polls, what people really believe.
How many are truly insane and blinded by the white disease?
A darkness that shines a black shadow on what it means
for twenty generations to sweat and bleed for freedom only to have it all reversed
by a throwback, ego-maniac, fascist fraud, cursed and begging for a bloodbath;
a replay of the civil war or worse, a global conflagration of the working class
against the new Amerikan oligarchs, bastards all.

The bigot base burns as this blue ball's tossed among those who must not lose
or face loss of face and faith and party to a torrent of tweets taken as law.
Face it, freedom is false and fried to a crisp at the bottom of the swamp where it's all talk.

Plymouth Rock, an extended arm. Shores and borders; smiles and arrows.
Progressive or Moderate; angry old man or shuffling old man.
Out and out lies or press bias, red allegiance a firewall against the people's voice.
No real choice without a real voice; peasants get the peanuts they avoid.
One chance to right the course of history, one vote per person allowed to be heard.
The virus votes to thin the herd and stop all vacations, vocations;
economic vigor lost for years.

We're all being tested but we can't get tested; everyone's testy and terrified —
Await words of warning without any warning and wait for breath to end.
Unemployed at the dawn of the apocalypse with a sore throat and heavy chest.

This recap is from frying pan and fire, rock and hard place, sweat, tears and blood.
The forecast is a recall; nudge off the cliff, down Alice's rabbit hole, the biblical flood.

It's COVID-27 I'm really worried about; overnight natural selection.
No rapture anoints the chosen.

A bear market shits in everyone's woods; dapper devil loses all talking points.
In Wuhan, bats hang in caves saturated with their own guano and rest easy.
No rescue net for those who don't eat pets; no more America if election's
postponed or stolen.
No more commute by bus and subway; no distance great enough
each alone to fight remotely.

Insurrectionist

I would carve the nails for his coffin, I thought.
Puma was licking corned beef hash off the spatula
as Capitol windows shattered; shards of lies
and dreams trampled on the steps
the very accusers of anarchy, completely consumed by it
smearing their shit on the halls of Congress.

I crack an egg with a bright orange yolk into sizzling butter
haunted by buffalo horns and face paint.
Tribal shaman of Trump trash declares shallow victory over himself
smashes his own windows in his own house
at the behest of orange Hitler false prophet
attempting Putin's planned coup
to satisfy a debt and keep the pee tapes off YouTube.

Life is funny and ironic but I'm not laughing.
"I want to voice my strong opposition to this impeachment - height of hypocrisy!"
rings in my heart
like a cracked bell that betrays a once true, ringing freedom.
A hearing of hypnotized, deaf congress becomes a Marvel good vs evil comic:
Gal Gadot leaps through the sacred halls, swinging from her golden lariat.
She slices off the heads of spiral-eyed Republicans
then faces off against the fat orange Nazi
deflects his lie-darts back to him with her magic cuffs!

Never has such a total loser caused so much pain and suffering for so many.
His own payback will be the ultimate bitch.
No one will suffer like he and his followers; it will be huge.
The most suffering in history
the suffering of suffering, the suffering of delusion
the suffering of pain, the suffering of loss.

What has it cost us?
One million dead.
Democracy in shambles.
Mother Earth in polluted pain.
Emboldened racists arming themselves for Civil War revisited.

What has it cost them?
We know who they are now
duped, delusional and dying.

Everything they stand for is lies.
A third party will kill the GOP.
Some oligarch will finally release the real pee tapes to get his yacht back.

The reckoning of the devil turns up the heat.
140 in denial and in a rush to revoke the republic
sit right back down, cross their arms, and vote to turn back time;
maintain the red lie at all cost, learn the tribal bleat
drag their feet, filibuster and fail at keeping their oath;
join the oath-keeper crowd fist raised.

The commission of this crime gets a limp Commission to find the truth.
So many fences to get stuck on, side-steps, congressional clocks run out —
Contempt met by dark laughter from the right.

2021 Recap: Apocalypse Phase 1

Pythagoras curls the weight of this vibrational shift with sacred geometry.
Sour music grates with potatoes and onion for latkes.
Turn your head from the year's stench, drop a dollop of sour cream
as above so below from Mariana Trench to Mt. Everest.
Greater than - Less than <> - empty brackets frame pandemic year three.

Weary victory denied, we become more weary.
Wary of everyone, not knowing if Red or Blue
or white reveals capacity for violence, lack of insight.
Crazy twist of logic such an easy wired bridge to cross
detonates at every step — So marks a path of destruction.

In the salumeria, lascivious grocer ogles my 12 yr old by the pepperoni rack
so I had him fired.
I lose my uncle to Trump lies and arrogance, bought and sold by blind bigotry.
Vaccinated and boosted, I hoist my ass up the stairs to work.
The best commute and highest rate I ever got, go figure.
I change agency and insurance and point of view;
returned my leased Infinity Q50, got a new black cat named Neko Yu.

We started with a coup d'etat and wound up with an artifact
of democracy so fragile it wept and muddled any call to action.
My Ukrainian dead urge me to war armed with forced memories of centuries evil.
I starved and got fat in my Titan gaming chair.
Took the risk on biologics and failed to tinker my skin DNA into a healing key.
Back to UVB, cortisone, and go easy on the Mortadella.

Wracked with doubt, on the edge, a dirty mask.
Dissatisfied with mailorder medicine, grocery run risk anxiety.
Apollo pissed; Thor's angry wind rises; Gaia depressed and aflame, gods overtaxed.
Hospitals packed with victims of the biggest lie ever told.
The spheres minor dissonance is a cosmic headwind.
We grow older only to repeat our grandparent's sins.

Through the keyhole with a booster, temporarily fearless
though we are not going anywhere, we are the 'Hangman'.
Locked in the house, we order *vindaloo* delivery.
Grubhub driver steals our *naan* and we get a refund.
There has to be a price to pay, phantom carrot hung.
One good kiss is all you need, two shots of Tito's
some sense that freedom is possible someday.

Simmer of unrequited hate aggregates into paranoid delusions.
All projects large and small are dwarfed by the unraveling;
what we feed the Eagle, manna of recapitulation hardtack.
Sad phantasm shot out of a neon cannon, a monster cloaked
in a backwash of protest against all direction except backward.
Spirits drop harder than the ball in Times Square.
Numb broadcast of old, unmasked entertainment loops
fails to fill the fracture; hollow, angry celebrations
can't stem the bloody year's bubbling pain.

*

Tanks roll along the border of Ukraine.
Billows of smoke roll down Main St. in Kyiv; animals scatter through the Lysa Hora.
Ahead of protests, thoughts and prayers abound in hapless naiveté.
Pale conscripts bound by madness crush the innocent with cluster munitions.
From Peruniv Hill you can see the ancient city scattered with smoking ruins;
170 prams defenseless and doomed.

Money flow swiftly stopped to isolate Putin & Co.
The sad, evil clown drags his people down
complicit to genocide;
makes them kill their cousins, homeless sick shatter of millions.
Nuclear sword rattled in hot rhetoric
by a madman lunatic fool and his minions.

Ragged refugees in shreds, wild eyes rattle in shelled skulls;
drag the contents of their broken lives
across frozen borders at night.
Dead *ruble* a sure sign 'The end is near'.
Faces strained in frozen masks of disbelief.
Everything that ends, ends in fear.

2024 Civil War Planning

Get the fuck out of dodge.
Dodge buckets of dumbfuck detritus cast out back windows
as doors are kicked in during Dayton 'Kristallnacht', Charlotte torch party 2.
Florida fire cannons sink into sand on collapsing water tables.
Vermont swelter in covered bridge sweatboxes —
Turn up the motorhome A/C, head further north.

Stop watching the news.
Nothing said has any bearing on anything whatsoever anymore.
Create a force field around your camp using
pop-up road spikes, slide out gun-pivots and gas atomizers.
Diving Red-tailed hawks trigger drone lasers.
Cameras feed the cloud with global surveillance.

Perspective being dead, bury a hatchet in its head.
A red serpent with forked tongue and no plan for Amerika.
A republic that is really a fascist oligarchy.
Oh my oh me oh my O maybe we can see a blue sky above O
O no more big lie O everyone is gonna die O.
Omicron is not the final mutation, they'll hit the front lines in rotation.

Put 2 and 2 together.
Stupid, delusional bigots want to remain stupid and delusional.
It makes you wonder if Charles Manson was right.
The 'skelter' forecast is more evil than we can possibly imagine.
If Trump wins again constitutional democracy will end.
Carve a "Z" on his forehead.
I repeat: Get the fuck out of dodge.
Check out land prices near Presque Isle.

A brook to fish, a sunny southern slope to grow staples.
Extra gas in the RV for ready escape to Halifax in a flash.
Cash in hand; supreme box organization, a brick
Daisy shot, extra sling, scuba fins, Lithium cells
notebooks, a chain of histories, childhood drawings —
All pasts pressed into a box and put away.

The nightmare is real; ready for violence, arms flail in the dark.
Echoes of escape by generations past fill the space
that was once a gap we could not imagine being filled.

Run from genocide, autocracy, exploitation, hate;
carry your diamonds, photos, silver and gold for trade.
Dodge is gone, don't ever go back to dodge.

Gather your papers, pay your taxes.
Generator on wheels, fluids, chainsaw, axe
any old motors, scraps of deerskin
telephoto scope, a couple of everything that fits.
Maybe that old first baseman's mitt, a few crystals
meds and liniments.

When words of derision turn to broken glass
no one left to be the guide, shine the light
none of us will be contained, we will all escape.
There will be no one left to dominate
no one to fight or harass to death
in a barren landscape struggling for breath.

Caution to the hot wind, reach the northern frontier.
Believe what you will, your tears will be shed and then
the salt will turn your cheeks a chalky white
below sunken eyes, above cracked lips.
Bleed, cry, suffer and die — Human ship of fools
dashed against the rocks.

The colors fade on every flag.
Believe what you will, your blood will be shed onto them.
The causes of criminal bigots stain those
that cannot allow themselves to care about them.
The people are told what they are allowed to know
and so the lies are sold as truth.
We are all betrayed.
Vicious dictators broil in their bunkers
bite cyanide teeth as the signals trickle away to static.

Weapons Of Mass Deconstruction

Weapons of Mass Destruction
in the khaki closet, blood stained braid & ascot.
Arms of dust under the bed, strange gas in the hamper.
Weapons of Mass Destruction
in the sugar bowl
behind the cat box; swords glint
under the washing machine, gassed to a pucker.

Weapons of Mass Destruction
in what you haven't said, what you withhold, what seems inevitable.
Lumbering dumb bombs & other shoes fall; acrid rain on patio wincing with hot ash
kicked up from a mean hickory BBQ.

Weapons of Mass Destruction prostrate at the pulpit —
Dark lessons in the shadowy apse after choir; lives ruined
with lies belched from a thousand dick-breathed priests
who eerily defend their abuse;
defend the fiery violence of a thousand crusades.
Weapons of Mass Destruction in thirty second spots
indoctrinating wave after wave of new consumers
into Amerika's last great urban plantation slavery-grave of drunken Capitalism!

Weapons of Mass Destruction where are they!?
We're at condition orange, we shudder with fission, the know-how to
trip Armageddon, steam released from a nuclear iron
that's got life white hot by the collar, hard-pressed to divert its dark course.
Fear the collateral damage to our hearts Amerika — fear your government!

Weapons of Mass Destruction — Invisible gases, minerals of death
mobile labs in the desert — Where!?
Sinister terrorists wrapped gut to gullet in C4 and 6 penny nails — Where!?
Overhead transformers hum, every bus, every cab, every subway car suspect —
        Satellite cameras shutter rapid-fire.
        Watch for turbans bearing fruit baskets — Where!?
        Watch for a thimbleful of virus; white powders in paste-up threat letters.
Find the AIDS needle in a stack of shredded homeless box homes.

Chain of targets like a blind conga line to oblivion.
Two million commute through midtown hit zone.
Beware the corner newsstand!

Beware what tries too hard to conceal itself.
Beware what pretends to try to be invisible.
Beware who doesn't try and obviates evil through stupid T-Shirts
of Osama in the bullseye or
"Fuck You You Fucking Fuck"!

These words are weapons
they dash a brick of catastrophe to dust.
These words are land mines;
sentences replace severed limbs to
fight for the world, pull it all apart and
re-hone our claw.

Polish up your glass eye Amerika!
Bear word weapons against Mass Destruction so fiercely
that no one would ever lift a hand
against another again.

Words are war.
This is a war of words
we worried masses
reject the argument for.

After War

Shards and shades pulled.
Shadow shapes haunt.
Middle of night sweats
persist.
Cold, ardent mint swirls.
Myna-bird Blitzer repeats
hearsay and rumor —
Wolves and red winds howl.

Tell it to the boy with no arms.
His stumps wave at the cameras; wave at ghosts, parents
who couldn't save him from harm.
Afterimage in a thousand pieces
he waves —
Insane MOAB alarm —
Daisy Cutter wrath splits ears, everything in pieces.
Broadcasted carbon fibers disrupt al jazeera puppet-dagger TV
reign in deep microwave sink hole to temper the blast.

Curry
disrupts
lentil;
the pot stews shrapnel, 'tooth for a tooth' broth.
Pumped puddles of crude slick and volatile —
Lakes of iridium
aluminum tubes of uranium
accelerate, concentrate, inner core of sun

gone ballistic
gone beyond reason
gone beyond ballistic disruption —
Mega, ultra, XXX, premium-channel, long-range

death.

Inverse hypocrisy embedded
inversely perversely personified

in exploded articulation of inset war-map desert caravan.

Satellite victory progresses
and deletes
from conscience
what remittance due.

Way Beyond Anger

Pursued at every turn by
some rage with a raincheck
that I stowed away
now back with a vengeance
and a penchant for
screwing myself
way beyond anger
into undealable disbelief.
No dealing with the
knockout punch of irony.
Is this all just
elaborate preparation for death?
Katie Couric seems to think so.

From Benghazi to Baghdad to Kandahar I am way beyond anger.
From Fukushima to Chernobyl to the Gulf of Mexico I am way beyond anger.
As a father, an earner, a taxpayer, I am
As a 'lonely man in the middle of something that he doesn't really understand'
As a rider, commuter, cubicle rat fighting for company kibble
I am way, way beyond anger.

What we defend
ultimately kills us;
the portfolio of successful jobs
the dusty black portfolio in the garage
the online portfolio
the multimedia DVD portfolio
the portfolio of horribly bad decisions
perfectly timed to be even more horrifically ironic
to screw myself as completely and deeply as I can;
to wound myself
way beyond an iron-on
way past a life-o-plasty
that masks some youthful folly
or carefree moments of oblivion;
to be spared one last misstep
to stem this tide of sadness
blinder this aching hunger
that reaches way beyond the boundaries of the fort.

Indian Point, built on a fault, is 30 miles from here.
I guess we'd head north if anything happened
but from there, who knows?
Wherever it is, I will be way beyond anger
no more would dancing bears make me smile.

I walk past the Army Recruiting Center, neon ol' glory
50 Ft. Nasdaq HDTV wraparound video wall
past the Good Morning America studio Euro-tourist 8AM Beatlemania screams
and I am way, way beyond anger; coffee spills over in the bag
soaks my ham and egg on an onion roll.

Arthritis, stenosis, domino row of root canals
carpal tunnel, Lincoln Tunnel, throw in the towel
dodge sinus-drain Port Authority hobble-stank crowd.
I am way beyond anger crossing Times Square
eye-migraine-blindered against Madam Toussaud and B.B. King.
No one carrying a Times anymore.
No one cares much about ink on paper.
iPod wired sardines play Gen Z punk to Superfly in caffeinated VR 3D hypnosis.
The voices of history exponentially multiply
until everyone has a voice in the social record
but no one can hear and understand complex thought;
no one can read more than 145 characters at a time.
Twits tweet crossing streets oblivious to traffic.

I am way beyond anger at inane urban bloggers
who turn the mundane view out their apartment windows
into purple cellophane universes; lots of crisp sexy noise, no candy.

I listen to the dead whisper toothy puzzles into a fish eye lens.
Their prismatic voices cry an inverse rainbow of beats and frequencies
being pulled smaller and smaller into a great mass of warning.
Fine hairs stand on end and burn for less than a nanosecond I'm told
as you are turned inside out like a tissue blown.

Now I know; they are my family, those voices
silenced in the Holocaust, with ringside seats for the rematch.
Both sides gear up for terrible loss.

They are my family, those voices
killed at Nagasaki, burned by knowledge, hubris, and device.
Passed-over survivors in their own way.

Put that on your iPad and tap it.
Kick that down the torrent and make it viral.
An alien server ODBC bridge uncloaks on the event horizon
our infant signal detected.
The earth shudders and makes giant waves.

Robots at the reactor report the radiation is way too high
for walking-dead scientists to bear.

2200 degree steam jets out from cracked concrete.
The city's damp heat smells of distant tornados.

Forsythia in bloom on Bear Mt. — My knee hurts, eyes burn with pollen.
Harley sounds freaking great though, heirloom tomato sprout bed in mold.

9/11 responders grilled as suspected terrorists
before getting their benefits.

Every bus ride is a potential explosion;
commuters moan by the side of the road while Rabbis gather flecks of skin to bury.

Every bridge and tunnel, targeted cloverleaf, outcrop of shallow-rooted locusts
all vulnerable to earthquake, hurricane, 747, scud, laser battleaxe, economic hack.

Woman drives her van off the pier by Gully's
kills three of her kids, the oldest, 10, survives.

Little Leibby Kletzky; Levi hid the boy's severed feet in his freezer
his little lost feet that fell into a monster's trap of madness and panic
dismemberment.

[MAYHEM!   A LIFETIME OF WARS!
        (A chorus of off-key horns —
1120 Ave. of the Americas sways back and forth as the blanket of mantle is
fluffed in Virginia, trees flatten in Craigsville, floods move neighborhoods
roads abruptly end at walls of rubble or lead into new lakes.)]

Freak poets care and hate what the world has done
and hasn't done to date.
The freaking world manufactures fear for compulsory sale
and we have no choice, we are led astray into freakdom.

I vote to wipe the slate; scrape the torrent with a new tracker
attract a swarm of responsible hackers and lizard-genius trans-human moshiach mensch
to warn aside another genocidal attack, lift arms and voices at once.

Too tense to bridge the rift in situational earthcraft, we escape slowly —
The latency of change-managed revolution.

I look at old photos from before the war, dwell on my great-uncles
imagine the conversations we might have had.

Their voices won't leave me alone
but I am too far gone — Way, way beyond.

SCOTUS Dumpstus

Scotus Dumpstus gave Trump a wall.
Scotus Dumpstus had a great fall.
The fall of Amerika has begun.
Cast the court as foe and run away.

Amy grimace foists the cross on all
In white-shouldered panic to claw back
territory lost to free people
happy in a warm melting pot.

Sam the secret man's man
hates the men's men and thus
himself; hairy hand-wringing
damned liar, hair & pants on fire.

Have another beer Brett.
Have a brat with the next one Brett.
God loves your croup
and your flop sweat.

Neil made a deal with the dark one.
Beneath his robe is a secret
thumb screw
on back roads
driving in short shorts.

Clarence plays POTUS patty-cake with Ginny.
Extends damp handshake to a billionaire
who buys his childhood home
to own him like a bond
that matures when he says so.

Scotus Dumpstus gave Trump a wall;
a small wall, migrants crawl over easily.
John, what you done, John?
Kids in infrared drop and run.
Abortion, Affirmative Action, LGBTQ freedom and opportunity gone.
With the swipe of a pen a chasm widens.

Supreme dumpster fire
spreads fast in the swamp.
Gases rise with the temperature.
Tinder box of the right righteous
takes only one spark from the left to blow.

Demon Commuter

Second Saturn Return

Get ready for a new kind of suffering.
Saturn soon four degrees away from my second return.
Step out into a new kind of light and burn away the fog
to see a real path for the first time.

Snowy woodpeckers dive, turn my house into swiss cheese.
Car slid down the icy driveway by itself in the middle of the night
with the emergency brake on.
I shop plastic owls with moving eyes.
The three times explode in retrospect
as I fill the holes with expanding foam.

Right now in this moment, this instant;
my one note
is a harmonic
and this is like
the moment you finally get a fire started
in the wood stove
steaks coming to room temperature.

Hello Prozac my old friend
it's hard to feel you come on again.
A warm fuzzy cap to my raw nerve.
A shield of neutrality for this Saturn return.
Face the corporate maelstrom stone-faced and in the zone.

Mechanism of stars clock the exact location
I will emerge from this stellar sheath.
I might be on line to board a flight to
a consulting job in Dallas or St. Pete.
I'll take the job as long as I don't have to suffer
the special linear torture of an Egyptian Operations Director
with a chip on his shoulder.

One step removed from
taking the full hit of the "truth";
this moment, right here and now
the fragile underbelly
of impermanence in all its ways
cannot be seen directly

but is a matter of avoidance
of what is too close to see.

Catch your breath at the turn of the year
push another degree away
from the harsh spotlight of pandemic fear uncertainty.
Support systems crumble in the rotation
like a tornado wrecks buildings in its path
destroys homes, businesses, hopes, dreams —
The letting go is what creates the past and opens the door
to a new market in which to spend.
Hard currency of experience on my face —
Heart dues come due.

The north node of the moon shines in her eyes.
Children gather round her in the 5th House.
We stand on the edge of the decade
leap into a headwind of stars
things that feel too far to reach
knowing that all stone crumbles and
you will be seen at any angle as you are.

Demon Commuter

"All the things in the world left to be done
by all the unfinished people in the world left undone."
— Louis B. Hirsch

I know who I am
but I don't know you
even though you brush past me daily
with your backpack
or bulging attaché
and all the working vacation
in the world can't hide
what burns beneath the surface of your
glazed, puffy eyes that track the
mass, repetitive fate of our
mutual demise
timed to coincide
with the expiration of our youth.

I don't know you
the dark bags you carry
the persnickety boss, the wear of
gravity, knees chafed by
seat backs, groveling and
fruitless weekend prayers to a god
that simply is not there;
as maddening as a crossword
missing a critical clue.

I don't know you
the answers you seek
the ups and downs of your
similar work week;
how you feel, hot or cold
the book, report, or cellphone
you hold, as the bus pitches forward
or the train slows
and the sky goes from
indigo to blue.

I don't know you
demon commuter, though our reflections merge
and paths cross

so my struggle to write this
finally must testify
to the death inside of all
that justifies the struggle itself.

If I knew you I might see
the perfect being that you are;
so perfectly in pain, anguished
by sun through hair grease blur
to temper the day's reflection
with blind glare and
turnpike congestion
buffered in memory by iPod
or suppressed by flu.

If I knew you
curled away, constricted
like a venomous snake
once awakened, ready to strike
with your entitled fang.
All rebellions rolled into one
dumped on my head
'cause my book bag is too big
or I belched lunch twice and
once was more than enough
or I smell like the stress you
thought you'd escaped at 5.

If I knew you
before you were soul-raped
emasculated, made mannish
by glass ceilings and tobacco
trained to revile the exploitation
and then to emulate
as you advance from one
of the crowd
to one of the elite.

If I knew you
red, burning eyes
breath poisoned and metallic;
you should have known
that I was a pretty big guy

when you took the seat beside me
and that my knee would stray
into your implied space
as I nodded off
but that just might trigger
some deep childhood fear
reveal some trauma
constricted and suppressed
school bus drama —
Hit by a bookbag
poked by pencils
tormented by gum.

If I knew
you had 3 hours sleep
a hemorrhoid as big as Kentucky
a boss who hates when you're late
a date with some big mucky-muck
a sister near a levee
a bum knee now crushed in pain
by the demon in the seat ahead.

If I only knew
your wife programmed the
whole night into TiVO.
You pretend to sleep
thrown against the window
while I mull my obsessive invention
'Commuter Survival Kit'
a link of adjustable padded, pocketed Velcro straps with
rubber coated clips that can attach
to the air vent edge
and wrap around arms or legs
to hold them pulled tightly in
against the growling pitch and yaw
of the diesel coach.
Well no such luck
you're gonna be late.
Your heart jumps
when you see a dead kitten
at the park & ride
surrounded by goose shit
and coffeecups.

If I only knew
how things persist
and things change —
Different arrangements
always the same
day in, day out
captive to the routine.
Empty books of ticket stubs
torn slacks in fast doorways
let in the breeze.
Neck crick, palm callous
sigh, dream, lie to yourself again today
about why you do it
why it has to be done.

Left alone with their careers
beaten down, beaten up
to clear the way to retirement;
clear the fear of never getting there
clear worry kleshas and wide-eyed Maya
clear threaded memories of pure fun
from way back when before computers.
Clear the way to the Lincoln Tunnel
and let us get there;
let me get there
and be done with it.

*

I know who I am
but it doesn't make it easier
or me less of a liar
and what I don't know about you
I can surmise by
laptop glow;
the way you play with your hair
your Blackberry.

Even with eyes forced shut
they open when I feel the spiral ramp
climb to Port Authority level 3
like a prescient vertigo to the days spin
and join the linear decent to the subway

pee, newsprint, humid sour grease of NY decades
layered everywhere.

City's fangs revealed by all the hairy reptiles;
sharp sweat in summer sun turned to vinegar.
Just being on our way in the maze
maddens limp discomfort past streaked tile.
An evil smile fails to conceal the scales;
the green tinge in your slit eyes
myopic to decay.

*

I know who I am but
we all forgot who we were
and forget who we are daily.
You let it all get to you
let the game dull your blade.
Score a new job
think you've got it made
only to find you still spend
as much as you earn
no cash to burn
and the chips are
stacked in a twisted politic.

Stress is cheap at each our own foreign-owned firm.
The rules change quickly
without notice or warning
and every other person on the road to ruin
is an idiot or a zombie
or corporate mercenary
or advertising genius
or pumpkin-headed teenager
a demon
who couldn't give a damn about
any other person
except himself;
who forgot who he was
supposed to care about
and what mattered
as he barreled down Rt. 17
in his red & white supercharged Mustang GT.

Muttering commuter paces like Groucho at the gate
dresses like a clown with a shirt whose tails
are too short for there to be a button over his gut

so it splits and doesn't tuck right and he spits on asphalt
curses his rut, tucks himself in at night with
a bottle of Jack and his own beefy mitts liquefied.

Pockets filled with mints and Pepto-Bismol
cinnamon Red Hots and crumpled chili-dog foil.
He ogles the girls, leans in to smell their musk as they pass in the aisle.

Frigidaire woman with a square face pretends disinterest
as you hush instructions into your cellphone.
Brackish icewater drips from the luggage rack A/C.

Nod off and make a swaying comma in the
sentence of rows that says how tired we all are.
Clutch that bag tight or it might roll away.

You too, gone in your own version of the news
gone suffering; weeks vacation doesn't even begin to scratch
the depth that longs to be revealed.

Atlas on quicksand holds up his family, upholds sacrifice
grinds a flying cockroach into pigeon shit
folds the Journal and slips it into kid leather

rolls up the window, turns up the radio
sees no – hears no – speaks no evil
bites the bullet of each rung as he climbs

gasping for air as he rises.

*

There'll always be a Don Blake to shake your ego with his petty tyrant rattle;
a Pat Little to belittle and deflect you as your project withers
an anal-retentive Tech Director who'll sit right behind you
and watch your every keystroke through the plastic keyboard protector
thin veil of distraction for a brain with such parallel processing traction
abnormal in its one-eyed tic mania.

There'll always be a Gary Blumberg to lie about bonuses
pretend to be your best friend then bend you over for the shaft;
a John Sagano to throw his thunderous heft around
vomit shrimp and lobster sauce on your desk
while yelling about something very small like a lost grounding strap.

There'll always be a Nancy McGraw, with fang and with claw to tear
at you under duress; a Steve Jacks heart attack stare, McLanahan reach-around
w/ side order o' jerk-ass Art Director shootin' bare blanks
or a Peter Grimlock to raise frivolous havoc and spank you
for the unintentional back-end-run-around to the senior V.P.

Operations *Mahakala* wrong about everything yet thinks he knows.
Production *Yama* fangs dripping blood and deadlincs.
Mobile ghoul on a digital dead man's race to app launch.
Red-horned editor, nose in a flaming iPhone.
All wrathful professions their own prison and demon mold.

Eyes dart in a thumb-lock grasp of the obvious;
to program the future needs a language not yet written.
This gap will be our undoing when we arrive at 21st Century Mt. Sinai
and look into the new chip valley below
we know we will never arrive to.

So many wasted geniuses lost in unworthy operating systems.
So few real chances to be and love what you do completely in unstressed flow.
So many greedy, evil and ugly people with ambitious agendas
filled with sorrow and unknowing, just looking to hurt you.
So many buses lined up day after day to be thrown under.

Black wind heat-wave chokes life out of the city.
Another badly written program chokes in the clinch
just when you need it to run.
Hot rain drains the colors from the gray street sewer halos
seen by Hippodrome bird's eye losing contrast in a sea of black pinwheels.

GLIOBLASTOMA

for Lee

Box draws tighter;
noose lariat thrown
wide around
a life and
drawn to suffering
and suffering's end.

Loss of the illusion is
the loss of delusion
and also the loss of
loss-tragedy; the tragic
loss of everything
and every single one
gone, gone beyond
a world insane and
growing more so;
so, now we know and
need to figure out
what the hell to do with all this loss.

OMA OMA OMA OMA
Blast it out with Polio
Stomp on it with giant suffocating radio-isotope boots!

OMA OMA OMA OMA
O Ma — Momma I'm-a
mad at life —
Made mad and blasted.
O Momma — OMA OMA OMA
O Brother — OMA OMA OMA
All of us dying.

I come out blasting
just like when Lee
stuck his finger in my
pop gun rifle and I
pulled the trigger
and blackened his nail.

OMA OMA OMA

Gave him his first hit of acid
my father playing guide
while grandpa died at dawn
as we came down.

I am constantly paying
for my karma —
No excuses.

OMAAAAAH! Blasted home in a
million pieces.

Blasted back in time.
Blasted with radiation through a laser hat.

OMA — Oh man not that
        not that not that not that.

OMA — *Tat Tvam Asi*
        I am that I am That I am THAT.

OM AH HUM!

Peace stolen in the night —
In the black beating pulse drum
hidden memories rise like
dark fish in a green pond haze.

OMA — OM AH HUM!

Glittering Glioblastoma!
Flatulent Glioblastoma!
Baroque and fuming tumor!
Critical mass overflow O-MA!
Glioblastoma go away!

Echo of OMA — Stereotactic nuclear ray delays the inevitable.
Eighteen months they say — OMA bargaining against terrible odds.
Poliovirus direct to brain asap — Can we give him
polio in time — OMA OMA OMA???

Bopped with a plastic
bowling pin on a Sheepshead Bay pier — OMA

Eating powdered donuts
on my stoop
at Ave. Y and 21st — OMA

I stumble through the
Village tripping
gripping the new Dylan LP — OMA

Surrendered to OMA
Hung out to dry in a cellular hailstorm — OMA!

I wish I was Indrajit
with a golden arrow
to shoot at orange Ravenna OMA!!!
From ten miles away my fission missile flies
in a giant arc of justice — OMAHHHH!!

Nuclear option — OMA!
Kill to cure allopathy — OMA!
American cancer profit center — OMA!

Avastin irradiated steroidal PET scan in stereo — OMA!
Choke off the blood supply to wild mind rampant growth — OMA!
Smoke mod vape pen mod with honey liquid death — OMA!

Buttery brain braises in poison chemo roux
a dracularian proposal to become food for an eternal destroyer;
fangs dripping with our blood in whitecoat racquetball dumbed-down conjob
a basket of shrunken heads holding open the sliding steel doors.

Faced with loss of self and words and wheel
stuck bargaining with faceless puppeteers;
a brake, a broken practice, practically useless
to stop this X train from its tunnel.

In days when these things don't go well
the future pulling in to your station of departure
we know we hold the rail with a billion others
all tired and hungry for home.

Whitetail deer and electric bears dance across the mountainside at sunset
on a surprise warm winter day after rain —

Home is always over there.

To Be Home

I drop out of the clamoring severe bottle-jam
tuckus-pounding cattle-car commute;
kick the brass bucket with a silver tipped Nocona boot
tip the horn forward like
a modern Coltrane in the subway
acknowledging coins tossed in his case.
He drinks out of a pocket-bottle every sixteen minutes
and immediately lights a Camel;
cooped up in the smells of bad wine
smoke, piss, puke, sweat and filtered street exhaust.

Methane in shuttlecar shaft, bixbite at the adit, all red rocks
of subway acid drone, masked by orange hat and call
of fruit vendor: *"Hey Straw-berry!" "Heyyy Berries!"*
Music too private to hear crosses past me on so many
little yellow "Walkmen," only a tinny backbeat merged
with clouds of railsmoke; a fight to the end, to be home.

Ching Chi

The glory of the essence achieved from one's
own indestructible nature
The taste of honey borne from the self-arisen body
This feeling from the play of a hundred thousand hairs
The tongues of gods in heaven have not tasted.
— Gedün Chöpel

Out with the old
and in with the *Yin* —

Bear claw buckle unlatched
with bare raw knuckle catch
of breath, clenched teeth
to steam our dual cultivation
"big draw" circulation of
Ching Chi passion waves rolling down
into the white sky and green water
of our valley orgasm.

Every drop of fluid
surging forward and back
in a perineal *tsunami* curl
retained to engage the *Tao*
on the most mutual and merged of terms
and greet each other's restful essence
with an open-eyed electrical sigh.

Bright red nails dragged across my back
leaving white trails I follow later;
great current of life filed and enameled.
Drawing pull of the root that conserves
hot milk chi-steam seed essence
ignites glowing belly coal that holds
the answerless *koan*; what we don't know of love
radiance that resolves and re-kindles
the mysterious light in her eyes —
Hot breath shared, surging to the crown.

Tongue pressed to palette links the circuit.
Round song of her skin rings harmonic
against my flexing pulse

rising spinal glow along
the microcosmic *chakric* orbit.

We turn together
like a prayer wheel —
Repeated meetings snap
like flags in a strong wind.
Hip to hip, breast to breast, eye to eye
loosened like a row of dark earth
turned to hold open for spring
and not conceal the sun
or suppress the rising steam
of a timely and
happy planting.

Two merging paths of bubbles;
fish rising to the surface of the stream.
One gull standing on a hidden rock
appears as water savior from Metro North AM nodding blur.
City streets drain the color, torque and essence
from lungs and eyes and a thousand old trenchcoats
blowing in a wind of two centuries *yin*-data *yang*-dada.

Waters flowing in the sewers retreat, fold over
their layered sheets of oily dust.
I take a Bass ale glow zither buzz arachnid stance
beneath a dizzy streetlamp.
Dull light drains the *wu wei* from this
carnival town seething art, sex, and death
my face pulled tight by a gritty East River chinook G-force.

Dark waters flowing through my arms, through my thrusting corridor
conquer everything; the alleyway is in me
embeds its coarse salt to my skin like a pretzel.
I am hard enough to make the Path tunnel come with echoing cries.
I am single-celled, one-track-minded
speeding toward the pickled egg of a Hoboken bar.

* *Ching Chi:* Taoist term for "Sexual Essence"

Urban Verses

Held by the city in this way:
Sweet Sofie Mang the cow-cat queen on
        left white sofa arm —
White cathair tumbleweeds
        waft across '40s parquet.

My own homemade pasta is
just as good as Pó or Il Cena Colo.
My ragu as sweet and savory
and it's Wednesday to boot
        'whatever' spaghetti day —
Come get your macaroni and gravy.

Held in this way
the city glows its steel edge
cuts through its own history
to immediate perfection
in every gray slice of life.

***

Woke my Reiki
on E. 21st St.
Soft gummy bagel
was the worst of it.
Could I be the key
to wake it up in you?

Noisy bakery
soft curl of almond smoke
imprisoned a la mode
within patterns on the back
of a croissant —

Wisdom books yellow and
universal symbols diminish
yet bad coffee can always be found
in some damp and musty bodega.

Reverse the polarity
and draw energy from this
grid — Every itch being scratched
every lid trembling around its
brief dream.

Sofie curls tight in
an Amazon box —
Empire State Building
casts a purplish glow
on her white fur.

***

Sun strobes on steering wheel
through silver winter branches.
Drive to the Park & Ride; take the Bus (Buspirone á la Shortline)
try not to get on the wrong line.
Jungle ramp mimics Port Authority mad slow escalator grunt —
Gray suited apes swinging from
painted steel rafters
to vie for the window seat that
reclines properly.

On the other hand, again and again
there's the Palisades dysfunction to the West Side Hwy
or the L.I.E. to Queens Midtown Tunnel
among other savage commute routes ever to rattle an axle.
Q104FM salvation a butter-salve for my
Hudson-Ganges infection
and tooth-gap Manhattan skyline pout;
missing teeth caught in my throat
again and again.

Jimi jabs his axe into my guts.
I rush decide to resign my package design IT job in Carlstadt
and take a more urban position.
Fear up the spine on first day of work — Sofa raconteur interruptus.
Mind in flight broadcasts a mayday.
Skycap oasis resonates like a Dodo.
Rival men raze Troy as the *schmatas* fly
extinct as Ratner's herring on Sunday.

You turn up your collar and the music
in your very expensive chrome earbuds.
Working for a living at a job that fails to satisfy
is highly overrated
except this mortgage here
says otherwise and Big Bank will wring you dry if you try to refi
so turn it up another notch
and pour me a double Gentlemen's Jack
and sit back on the couch.

I think of Joe Roberto
biker friend lost on 9/11 in One World Trade
as I put my bike away
for another winter, dirty.
I wonder what exactly he is missing really
in this city
          in question now
as is this
elusive anxiety

suppressed by a bagel with Nova and a schmear
twice a week for 38 years!

Two dark squares in the concrete waterfall
as freedom tower skin's applied
and we lift from our knees at the wall.

New York City is its own antidote
self-liberated.

Meanwhile, holiday cards still arrive
at 10048 phantom post office
for those ghosts that time and discount Bulk Rate
will not surrender.

***

Insurance, man
insurance is what gets me;
it just gets to me, you know insurance?
Man, it just gets to me
you know? You know insurance;
you never know they say —

You never know when you'll
need it but damn, insurance
that shit just gets to me
runs in the family.

My grandparents, father, not insured;
not a penny maintained to sustain a legacy.
After all, these city streets were
paved with gold —
Mica flakes in dark concrete shone.
So many little and big lies twinkled
there on the street
in between gum spots
and cigarette butts.

Concrete slabs wired to the teeth now
in Greeley Square.
They know your shoe size
and what you had for breakfast as you walk through.
There are no guarantees
at ground zero.
Strange lights glow
from Korea-town
manholes

and I'm hanging on insurance; I'm just
hangin' on and layin' low, trying not to
anger the premium and further harass the underwriter.
Only undertakers triumph as children fall to assault rifles.
Bloomberg collects a gun a day so Mort Zuckerman can preen
his hat's half feather with a half-page feature.

Tempt fortune and fate to temporarily evacuate the superstorm.
Gravitas envelope descends and the Mayan calendar defends its apocalypse
in the face of subsistence existence being forced upon Brooklyn.
A tri-state tsunami decimates Staten Island and
mold emerges victorious.
Only insurance separates the family
from their home.

9/11 vets chorale around the Christmas tree memorial
as bulldozers push their homes into mountains of
lost memories and identities.

***

Baked yet hardly awake
Farley post office lines are comet tail streams
among the facade scaffolds
and we are falling dust —
Little bits of citizens being found
in sewer grates day to day
years after the towers collapse.

Gray steel wing flap lift, hidden faces found at the foot of
a gray mosque alley trap, burned gray matters to ash —
Turned beards grayer to sift old cells
through the gray dust at Park Place.

That day — That day...
I saw the towers fall from my 51st St. office window
held on to a file cabinet as my knees buckled —
Ran down 15 flights of stairs and got my car as sirens blared.
So amazed at the goddamned fucking West Side Highway
a totally empty, mid-morning barren ribbon to oblivion.

For a moment shocked to be alone in my escape;

made it to the GWB in about six minutes
that day —
Rubbed my eyes
and the goddamn traffic reappeared again like magic!

The bridge was closed so I looped around on 9A and
when I hit it again it was open outbound only —

Holy fucking shit! I thought, banging on the steering wheel;

they will give a pilot's license to just about anybody!

Holy fucking shit! I cried
as I curled onto the empty Palisades;

they will give a driver's license to anyone
nearsighted or far
and anybody can
blow themselves up

but I swear
my brakes
and broken heart
are not the same
since my Palisades escape

that day.

***

Cannabis detox to climb the job ladder
scrubs old resin from brain
leaches from fat into pee.
I jitter and fret, purge and sweat the interview.
Mannaquin pose stone face dictates your fate:
"we regret to inform you sir
but you are an old gray
pothead and cannot be trusted."

So why not open a gourmet food market?
Maybe a rock shop or hobby depot?
Stock Radio Shack electronics experiment kits
lots of stuff to solder together and shit.
This lapidary, poet-chef sings a gray blues
slings sizzling hash in tune.

Cast your jones in the Harlem River
like a dark lure
and be in good company.
The muck and mire
turns under and rolls out to sea.
Learn now the ladder leads nowhere man
at least nowhere you want to be.

Gonna quit my job
oh yes, that's what I'm gonna do;
gonna quit and move uptown
to another job that I'm gonna
wanna quit too —

Alas, poor me — Pulling six figures
and miserable as a chocolate chip cookie
on a china plate

everyone diabetic all around me;
sick of me
and my spicy ham & egg on an onion roll.

Late for work and lovin' it
cayenne pepper sauce on my mustache —
Later I will blow it burning out of my ass
and think of you
old thorn in my side for whom I sacrificed
my true Broadway calling
for a string of kiss-ass peon jobs for peanuts.
Subtle doom and daily struggle;
keep up or fall
beneath the wheel
pay through the nose, skinned at the knee
given an arm and a leg
a delirious amputee.

[This poetry is a rescue
from the death of all dreams.]

***

Craigslist monkey hoots his crazy beef;
'Rants & Raves' get sad and lame.
The bargain you thought you gained on that USB board
turns sour when his UPS tracking number
is bogus as a purple dollar
and you want to put him in traction.
Your red face bleeds grief
for each and every 'Missed Connection'
each plight as common
as an arcade token
bent in a jimmied slot.

The shakedown continues
as the streets of April
turn hot and the pickpockets
come out of hibernation
to twist their elbows into
finger hooks and hand blades
squeeze into packed subway cars last on
to lift the cash you just made.

Brushed by on the street
by someone who
obviously knew
where they were going.
"So what" I say, they're deluded
and we all share the same delusion
so it basically works

yet not too difficult to see through
chinks in the armor
dreams in the gutter —
Sour gust heads north to some suburb or another.
Runs in cheap nylon distracts you at the curb.

They put up a shiny new sign
at the corner hot table take out
and scraped off the
health dept. stickers —
Still, you eye the black beans suspiciously.
Desiccated pale parboiled bacon strips
and pre-prepared egg whites on a silver tray
like plaster frozen on a trowel
fail to appetize
nuked on demand
for scary FIT undergrads
in very tight underwear
who always look like they're arriving
at a goth picnic with a bag of melba toast.

***

Max Parrish photo barks from
wrought iron kiosk —
Mismanaged buildings crumble
and spark.

The furriers eat peanuts
and florists stack tulips
in long waxy boxes sporting windmills.
Three steps away
a homeless guy wretches
into a trash can.

Old bulldog squats
on a subway grate to poop.
Pink hairy dog boner
wags in R train wind.

Outside Mickey D's
the guy makes unintelligible, snide comments to me.
His stench combined with
greasy burger and bulldog shit
enough to make me
drop my Post
blanch pale and dizzy on
26th and 6th.

I swallow this tender weakness
this humanity
over and above all fragility
bemoaned
as it is left to us
and must be made
less hollow
like the icy wind that
gets under my gray wool coat
no surprise and yet   ~ oooohhh ~

To hold that poise
an instrument for winds
that race down 7th Ave.
is to crack the monster minor 7th
of these blues —
Smell burger and
turn corner
back to the wind
and a
brighter step.

Evening walk destination: 34th St. Herald Towers apt.
in old Hotel McAlpin
where fifty years earlier my father had his first
secret dates with my mom
upon whom the disapproving "'50s" could
find no hold

when the city was a mere 7.7 million of us
in line with debonair ruffian Lindsay;
pre doom and gloom, in between the waves
of chaos, tide of grey coats rising
toward Penn Station.

***

Two pigeons peck a kernel of
unpopped popcorn into traffic.
I ran over a white one the other day
           — Puff of feathers
in the rear view — Did a *mantra*
or two but I didn't feel bad
inured to daredevil pigeons that plunge
into midtown traffic.
           Allen would say 'open up to
  raw warriors heart! — HUM HUM HUM!'
  Maybe someday I'll get it.

Coos from the window ledge
wake me from a dead sleep.
I walk downtown over
bouncing basement doors.
Rats dance in cardboard kitchens ankle deep.

***

Old webs bind me
into a numb chrysalis
await my rebirth
at some later re-emergence.
City's insomnia
keeps one suspicious eye
on all who aspire
to change
or arrive to the party late.
Sirens chase us
back into blackened doorways
wings folded.
Taxi headlights are eyes
like gems that blink and flutter
with each pothole and metal road plate.

Steel trashcan of old lunch bags
bursts into flame
draws us out
into the night again
to attain
fractured flight
and pull free
finally.

***

Walk and call, traffic through Times Square slows to a crawl.
Sidestepping Mickey, Minnie, Mario, and Buzz to get to the bus.
Tune out bible stumper Jesus-fuss and a hundred tourist cellphone cameras
that click everywhere to capture that New York angle
only to paint targets on their own backs
scammed on hot dogs and cab hacks detour through rush-hour park tangle.

Walk and text and call; even with "LOOK" epoxied into the street off the curb
some cannot tear their eyes from their smartphones.
Trucks and taxis growl down 8th Ave. inches from impact.
So much more disaster is averted than we realize.

Need to wake this small mind from its charmed oblivion of steel and glass
and heal the cracked hearts and streets of the city. [*Dai Koo Myo*]
City that bleeds and rumbles and moans.
City where I was born and that I am proud to call my home.
I hear the low frequency rumble of echoes buried deep below cobblestone.
I hear the bleat and blare of tragedy taking corners too fast
and pieces of desperate reasoned conversations that waft
from backpack cafes and alleyways, wisped thin as the job trail fades.

I am the first one in to work these days.
I eat lunch at my desk with one hand on the mouse to keep my seat.
Cracked economy keeps us walking and texting and calling and not looking.
Held by the city; the sonic, sacred, scarred, and nascent city.
Walk and text and call and cut through the small talk —
Just walk or just text or just call and that's all!

Mask of rage and fear please fall away;
let it complete, ease and dissipate
          — Resolve into *Maitri*.
May work anxiety dissolve into "Just don't know".

May money fear release into “Just don’t care”.
May I someday stop hating my ex-wife;
she got hers, you got yours, everybody got theirs.
May those I love find their balance in life.
Walk away from hate, numb and weepy
stoned or straight, nobody cares.
Walk with your heart on Earth’s stellar shirtsleeve.
Everyone you meet is your rebellious child and mother
designed to be loved and tamed by giving wide berth.
Walk through Times Square whirlwind open-armed
stripped of pretension and innocent faith.
Walk to the corner of 42nd & 8th
and become enlightened by the 10,000 *dharmas.*
Till your ‘maters and your peppers like a good suburban farmer.

Walk 500 lives as a fox in a state of grace.
Walk as a child of illusion tempting fate.
Walk ‘til you simply cannot walk any further.
Time changes your face into stained glass;
losing self, gaining self, it all comes ‘round again at last.

Walk ahead though you’d rather wait
or run and hide in the park like Jonah in the belly
of a great whale, lost in the gray noise spell.
Live in muddy water with purity like a lotus.
Let it all go and just be exactly as it is, block by block

and sure enough the dark gray sky
opens up.

Train to The End of The World

Metro North platform like a wailing wall;
survivors stand heads bowed waiting
for the train to the end of the world.

Parking lot now half-filled, yellow ribbons tied to antennae on cars
abandoned
by commuters who never came home.

Crematorium ash drifts uptown on a sour wind;
the migraine that wouldn't quit.
The bond trader back at her desk by 7 AM the next morning
gags on a buttered roll.

Root canal of city tooth labyrinth.
Vicodin sway trance across 7th Ave.
holding my jaw in a numb jut.

I hop the 'N' two stops to 49th
stare at sheet music in Colony's window
avoid the office a few more minutes.

A hollow echo down the tube
as the falling column roars —
Here I am boarding the train to the end of the world.

The PATH is rough, flooded and treacherous.
Fly a flag, wave a knife, steal a plane, sift gray mud for body parts.
Busy desk a mountain of rubble, recession's blinders on.

Will I reach the promised land with my children?
Will I accomplish the thought, word and deed, voice of peace and security?
Will the tassel be torn from my shoe, jammed under the
        opposing seat of this foursome?

Will I be late for that early meeting?
Is my beeper dead? Is my Palm Pilot alive
        where I have crashed?
Lights flicker and rails squeal past Christopher St.

Cold Blue

for Joe Roberto

Corn flowers brush blue sky.
Dew splash as weighted leaf
bends to flow.

Blood and honey stick to shades.
Where is Isis? She got out —
AWOL chasing birds.

Iron gone cold — Chrome in shadow.
To be loved and to travel — To show
a wristband and gain entry — To

walk on Pine Lake beach picture postcard
eating blue licorice
midnight Sept. 11th, 2002 —

Faces and names read
drop like bombs on our eyes.
Tears fall to rubble;

the many things that remind me of you
shards of beams
steel bone dust.

Over the Hudson Once Again

Straphanger's blues on tiny earphones;
digital cellular dingalings can't get
    enough workday.
Loose suits and lips at 7AM;
caffeinated cackling hens
recount burnt toast and soccer practice.
Action unending day in, out, otherwise —

Over the Hudson once again.

Tunnel maze, feint urine aire, empty box splayed
with someone's lunch rotting in a dark pool
between the rails.
Damp tin bezel a cankersore on the mouth.
Rushing must echoes through WTC
like stale breath; a thousand closed eyes bounce uptown.
Best to hide in the closed circle an open Times provides;
insight in crossword cops out on the one misnumbered clue —

Over the Hudson once again.

Pound that Palm, Handspring, stylus poised, block out time,
move the Ace of Diamonds onto its Solitaire pile.
Blackberry radio email a sure way to stay plugged in;
thumb wheel click yourself into a ragu of red digits.
Infrared beam me those figures and your V-Card.
Slotted cradle, one button, five minutes and you're downloaded.
You travel across the mainframe in milliseconds, eight hours later —

Over the Hudson once again.

The banana, the yogurt, the Basic 4; the cinnamon bun
the latte, the oatmeal, the Krispy Kremes, the bagel and cream cheese
the sausage and cheese, the bacon and cheese, the soft scrambled
    with lettuce and ketchup
the almond croissant, the Earl Grey, the Starbucks — Giant percolator gleams
on cheap white porcelain cup; bitter coffee, how many I forget.
The Morning Sunrise muffin, the baguette — Lavatory car door sticks —

Over the Hudson once again.

Sandwiched, shoulder bags at issue; run out of town on a rail.
Too much Chanel; too familiar strangers persistently chill.
Grey pedophiles chat up an 18 yr old International Business student from Brazil.
Anxious and indignant woman insists upon holding a large wrapped oil painting
on her lap which digs into my knee, makes a scene, attracts wrath of the car.
Lunacy repressed by chatter, Game Boys distract; lap top DVD rentals chirp
and sigh in private theatres two feet wide. Head and eyes roll back —

Over the Hudson once again.

Perfect Day

Only on imperfect days
will you be unable to explain
what love occurs to you on a train
as you travel from the city
all bundled into your vinyl corner
head fallen back onto the seat
mouth slightly open, thumb pressed in to hold
a favorite page in Rilke's sonnets
        "as though it already were
        behind you, like the winter that has just gone by."
A history ahead of all parting
her image already gone like a song you must hear every day
forgotten again and again
at that
        "infinite source of our inmost vibration"
as though it already were a memory.
Looking over at her
a music perfect in every way
        eating chocolate, reading whatever
knees both pushed up tight into the
back of the seat in front of her
and behind, the rushing, red-lipped towns of New Jersey;
Hohokus, Ramsey, Mahwah —
Her reflection in the plexiglass imposed on that motion
more than just light passing around blond hair;
face forgotten again and again as though it already were
true as Orpheus was a true muse to him
and she is now to me
colliding with my silences
alternately with the lyre.

The Price You Pay

"We must finally recognize the price we are paying to maintain the iconography of our ignorance."
— Sam Harris

You pay for your fear —
It's madness to think it has no bearing; you clamp down, you're useless, you uproot the tree to save the fruit, nothing feels good, cold sweating pale and dizzy, overstoned twisted knee compressed Shortline commute. Crippled dodge down the escalator and what for? The ice melts slowly and as color returns to your face you realize your pocket's been picked. It's gonna cost ya. 87 in a 65 ticket on the way to the park & ride so we're talking 300 bucks to the lawyer for starters. You are fined for your fear, penalized for regret, incur fees beyond reason and a testicle deficit in kangaroo court.

You pay for your love —
Does it pay to cry over spilt milk? Is it in man's nature to rebuild a broken nest? The housewren barks angrily at my proximity to her porch-hung home. She don't like me today; what can I do? Buy something new. Fine silk and fatty tuna; kid gloves and back rubs, endless chores and loud snores bracket ecstasy in stark reality. Communicate and pay; don't communicate, you pay more. Life sucks being alone so go for broke.

You pay for your hate —
It eats at you and makes you pay the check, makes you a nervous wreck, fleeces peace and breaks the energy bank. A thankless vengeance persists; the pompous schmuck that got my Amazon seller account suspended — Aaaargggh, I wanna kill that guy! All for a pittance $4.95 CD he says I bootlegged but I didn't. Pity, I have to pay for the other guy's stupidity. Isn't it always that way? Dumb-ass people make you pay.

You pay for your home —
Each picket in inventory, each wood screw, each and every gutter screen, and tube of crazy glue. Gooey asphalt patch and a tamper; gooey asphalt patch on your new suede moccasins! Oh fuck what did you do? Temper, temper, everything gets a good going through; you just go through everything then don't you!? Projects left undone for decades; vanity, base molding, sink, faucet, countertop, mini-split AC. Deck stain a major pain in every way.

You pay for your pets —
I stack tuna cans like poker chips. A silo of birdseed. Twenty years is just too short a time for a cat they really should get thirty-five years or even more. Got a cellphone call on Harley vacation at a gas station in Vermont that Isis died and Neisha girl put her in the freezer till we got back and cleared space amid the roots of a big maple for her bones. Clone-a-pet gets my vote; reckless genetic engineering of a super-cat is my first task post-singularity. Every twenty years I lose a piece of my heart; that's gotta stop.

You pay for your technology —
You're slowly being eaten by bacteria. Radiation glare eclipsed by swarms of nanobots. Mt. Everest brought down to size in a wafer of DNA computed simplicity. Billions and billions of computations per second later; the curve rises to dizzy heights. Borg and X-Men are born in deeply hidden labs; identical sheep on rolling leas of green grass munch cud at the same pace. No one gets credit. Cash only at the replicator. No mercy in the metaverse.

You pay for your dangerous fun —
Reach into the kitty and throw all the money at the Harley; ALL the money at the Harley; all the *MONEY* at the HARLEY! The left rear directional is not grounded and is always hot, always lit. Sound familiar? Needs rewiring. There's a short. Rear tire's bald, cough it up. You pay by the mile; you pay like an open wound, you pay to keep up with snarling wolves nipping at your ass halfway up a chain link fence. The tolls keep hitting your psychic ez-pass; you pay for every ride, every casual side-glance, when you least expect it and some mysterious force pushes you over the edge like an orgasm spasm of abandonment to skill and tooth skin. Chrome blindness close calls can cost big time. Tighten that weight belt another notch.

You pay for doing drugs —
Fifty years of pot smoking won't win you any prizes but hey, life's tough and you need a buffer from the pain. Yes concert, early 90s — Someone just said my name three rows back. I heard it loud and clear like they knew me; I swear I heard it — Jon was singing "South Side of The Sky"; it was getting really loud and the arena spun round and round like it always did but we got too self-important and serious about it all to enjoy it, holes in both pockets. It all started with pink dyed saccharin on line at Carnegie Hall for Monty Python Live that filched my last twenty. Cat ate the last crop when only an inch high. Little shit! No harvest, no payoff. Now my medicine is delivered on Thursdays.

You pay for the right to bear children —
Chemistry set of hormones wreaks existential havoc on the universe. So what; are you going to be the one to tell 600 million years of evolution that the rules suck? Yeah, you have the right but is it right? Jam an oil spout in your chest and emote till you're blue or be the bad guy. Never mind, you'll be the bad guy anyway. Svengali ex-wives twirl their evil mustaches and plot their next free ride. Twenty years later, you still have a beautiful child.

You pay for the privilege of raising children —
Who knew best? Who knows? She pays her student loan; the money always shows up. Your life lands in your lap and sits there; that's all it does honey, it just sits there while the meter runs. You have your funs, you pays the piper. The glow fades and ripens into well-considered and measured tones that attempt to gently persuade. In time, memory fades but irony does not.

You pay for your lust —
Steam shower womb glistens with all desire surrendered. Don't let the spam get to you; you did, you let the spam get through didn't you? You failed to stem the tide of spam and you just succumbed; you did, didn't you? You clicked it; I know you did, you clicked it. You dropped your coins in the slot and you pulled real hard; you pulled real, real hard but you couldn't come. No pop-ups, No pay-off. No bleached inbox, scrubbed history.

You pay for your hobbies —
It would surely trouble you to discover that there were four original 1969 Star Trek episodes that you had never seen. This news might actually stop your life cold in its tracks. You might also be shocked to find out who really stole your collection of Lincoln pennies and Jefferson nickels from the safe at the Roosevelt School. A basement full of rocks, a box of old Lampoons from '73. A closet full of expensive cowboy boots that hurt your knees. Tighten patella strap Velcro please.

You pay for your troubles —
Eventually no one wants to hear them; they pile up as jagged memories you shy from, the miter vise tightens on your left ball. Woe to those whose woe imposes. Blah, blah blah won't buy you 20mg. of Prozac in this town boy. There are people running from missiles over there; you get three square. Everyone pays through the heart. No one gets out without a fight. Pandemic poverty, fragile sanity, senile calamity, surreal reality chips away. Massage gun on my neck blurs sight to a seizure.

You pay for every grimace, every wince —
If it hurts it hurts that's all. Buck up you fuck-up. You pay for bucking up too. Pay up! Fuck you, you suck; you fucking suck, stop hurting me, stop it! My big giant maw is coming to take a $47,000 bite out of your house and turn your life upside down, now pay up! The refrigerator's broke, the carpet's stained with pee — Pay up, pay extra, pay till your fingers bleed and your comic book eyes roll kaching kaching. Buy a new coffee machine, a crystal figurine. Ration the Oxy and Gabapentin.

You pay for your indecision —
It's costing me, it's really costing me; wracking my brain to find a good reason, letting years pass without surety as to what actually, truly matters in this pitiful, violent world. Can't we all just get back to the Eden we know it can be? Shit or get off the pot; live by faith or by doubt. Cast worry to the wind and be here now or spend every last second heading for the precipice of a flat universe. Choose or lose. Vaccinate and risk enormous balls or die gasping for air. No brainer for a no-brainer.

You pay for every single chance lost —
You win some, you lose some. You win some; you win some, you lose some, you lose some, you lose some, you lose some, and you lose some more. You're baked fresh daily and you're a loser. You buy high and sell low; you've got the leverage of a plank

of dried lasagna. Your stock is worthless paper; you're all tied up in existential assets. Profits lost chip away at some idealized self-image. Grains of sand funneled into the furnace. Everything is slipping away from itself, each moment unrecoverable. Nothing stays suppressed for long. Regret is a stain with no solvent.

You pay for your war —
Currency of stumps and dark corners, post-traumatic, paraplegic, change dispensed with swift severance. "Here, I'll trade you these here thirty strong-balled younguns in exchange for that there secret formula for global annihilation, but you gotta take those sixty-two broken bodies over there off my hands; out of mind, out of sight behind that drawn bloody curtain. Sweeten the deal with this here eighty gallons of plasma, and I think I can persuade the general to up his price to include 8 captured women and a humvee." Boxes of bones, fifty gallon drums of blood, Tigris a river of gasoline. *Katyushas* at discount. This is the price of faith; bloody borders forever.

You pay for your god —
You tithe your mind to an idea of a divine being who wrote a book. The only book that explains everything. The only book that costs you everything. The book that counts every action in every moment of your life and examines your pleasures with suspicion. This strict accounting leaves you in poverty. The books of evidence are not balanced. God is not my fault. God is never at fault. There isn't any no-fault insurance against theocracy. You are liable for the complete lack of evidence. It is the highest price you will ever pay. Swollen Roman coffers aside, the church sanctioned every genocide, and on the other side there is no paradise, no virginity unabused. No pay off.

You pay for your excuses —
There is no defense against anything. Nothing quantifiable to defend. Period.

You pay for gravity.
You pay for the superheated plains.
You pay a dear, dear price and dig even deeper
at the American dream mine where few fortunes are made.
You call the bet and face the ultimate raise.
You're bought and sold before you even know the price
and the peanuts, samolians, sawbucks, c-notes accumulate.
Stacks of gold coins in a safe no hedge against apocalypse.
Invoices pile up in the queue;
debt stress panorama lights up like Washington beneath a Cohiba.
Wrapped in cellophane, each breath crinkles and folds
like your big stack of bills beneath the bridge
where it's all water under
and your short stack of bills behind the fridge
for the occasional bender.
Blew 60Gs in scrip at online poker.

Got taken to the cleaners, held upside down and shaken
heavily taxed and rarely rebated
so Bush can buy tanks to kill Arabs.
We pay endless mornings as we cross Port Authority bullseye
and our parents cry and our children cry
from the cost of religious need to be free of habit.
Habitual wallet hemorrhage in need of relief.
God, can you believe the price of beef?
A Franc a Yen a Buck or a Pound
you can eke out a living or blow Euro brains out
you'll still be bled dry eventually
and pumped full of formaldehyde
which you'll pay for
posthumously.

Can't Say A Thing

Can't say a thing about old legal pads with poems that I can't recognize.

Can't say a thing about spa temperature relative to Ph.

Can't say a thing about elderly parents that won't take their meds and are rushed to the ER talking gibberish.

Can't say a thing about Cambridge Paving Stones, or Farxiga, Latuda, Stelara, Victoza, Xarelto or Xeljanz.

Can't say a thing about the fact that I love Jesse Mai Lotus for ever-n'-ever.

Can't say a thing about my music heroes all dying, and even worse, playing badly.

Can't say a thing about feeling helpless and unable to alleviate my mother's suffering.

Can't say a thing about falling apart and being in pain.

Can't say a thing about taking a fistful of methadone, morphine, Xanax, Celexa and potassium.

Can't say a thing about anxiety and bloody cuticles and the smell of liquid bandage.

Can't say a thing about saying the wrong thing and being unable to take it back.

Can't say a thing about survival rates, or blue lips, or what it's like to have a heart attack.

Can't say a thing about hospital rooms or the alcoholic indigent next door getting maggots removed from his feet.

Can't say a thing about the moment when a lifelong caretaker becomes frail and the one needing care.

Can't say a thing when families age, change, die, fracture and evolve, becoming new families.

Can't say a thing about a creative person's decline into old age and death.

Can't say a thing about tears streaming down faces.

Can't say a thing about a family in crisis.

Can't say a thing about loss and letting go of love and what is real and never lost.

Can't say a thing about how to face the unknown.

Can't say a thing about riding 600 miles around the Finger Lakes in scattered thunderstorms and 98 degrees screaming and crying at an imaginary god through S-curves.

Can't say a thing about a beloved cat with a urinary blockage rushed to the vet and catheterized.

Can't say a thing about three job offers all arriving in hand at the same time after seven interviews each over four months of delays and no talk of numbers.

Can't say a thing about the iPhone 7 Home button.

Can't say a thing about becoming a novice monk and sitting in a small cabin on a mountaintop.

Can't say a thing about the Pirate Bay and 10K saved on movie tickets.

Can't say a thing when a mud bee clogs up the muffler on my leaf blower.

Can't say a thing about the endless list of things to do like drops in the ocean.

Can't say a thing about a box of old pornography from the 80s.

Can't say a thing about a potential Trump/Christie ticket or pinkys high at a poison tea party.

Can't say a thing about the mess we've made of our country or the enormous risk we are all at.

Can't say a thing about being silent.

Consultant Enemy

#1

Anonymous email from
god@heaven.com
tells you how much
even after four years
you are despised.

Petty tyrant triggers
inevitable high blood pressure.
Unreasonable stresses
guised as extraordinary results.
90-day bonuses just another
of your excellent bold-faced lies;
so precise, so strategic, so satisfied.

Page me at 11:30 at night
you bastard — Go ahead.
I drill a small hole
in your laptop battery;
power gel leaks out with your brains
at 5 AM Powerpoint launch prep.

If my revenge distresses me
it is only because everything
you stand for is abhorrent to nature
and I have stooped down to
your Best Practices.

#2

A face lift
for each of your
two faces
could not smooth
the wrinkles
each one has earned
and given to others
in return.

A hardnose lesson taught
about how to fire
a non-performer
for not knowing
all ten secrets
of paperclip utility.
Dangling carrots of business glory;
gold bar deeply bends the bow.
This process schedule
toward success
loses value
the more you know.

#3

The “end state” you prescribe
image of where I must ultimately be
to meet your unreasonable needs
a robotic technical resource
not quite human
        is an executive abomination
over pizza and beer.
Lunchline threats assure
mutual whiteboard destruction.
All your autoboot apps loaded
in cascade of spreadsheets, databases
and memos reveal
an heir apparent to the lizard throne.
In a binder, a deck, the proposal
map of a coup, golf course butter-up
slicked back chop chop house cleaning
“…you — and you — and You…
                                        OUT!”
Seventy hour week ends
and you are very clever indeed;
the people soft, the soft Peoplesoft charade.
Lotus Notes front end masquerade terminates
the programming of a database routine:

If
        the global temp pool slurry >1
        case(blondbraid=“perk”,

independence and vitality for life="0", "")
Else
Exit Script.
End If.

#4

Dry cough tic
huddled with smartest management.
Drop kick a workforce
invest in the thick of it.
Gain the moloch, lose argent arbitrage.
Gain the deed and colophon, lose your
right hand pages, your stories.
Gain the red-eye to Lima, lose
colloquial scientific humor
and make it plain — To attack me
only sends me to prayer.
When you hate me, is it for
the button I pushed or the thought
I may have been right?
Revenge — isolation — revenge — regret
lope of heavy rhythm defiles
defines the dark cloud that follows you.
Road rage on Rt. 80, an evil smile
not so well defended
after all.
Gain or lose, it's the way you bring your
shoulders back for the swing that
titillates the Ocelot.*

#5

Placed clearly beneath
such magnanimous beneficence
is a nesting instinct so behemoth
and wary of intruders
as to merit an array of electronics
reinforced and super-aware
of all irregularities.
Stand on your back porch

with a shotgun, listen
for rustles in the brush
heart pounding with fear
insane with hesitation.
Stalking small game in
the backforest cubicle.
Constant monitoring of
every situation, a questionnaire
rated on a scale of 1 to 5
and responses all graphed in charts —
Whose sacrifice reigns supreme
and who will cauterize
the wounds of personnel?

#6

Acrid coffeeground slurry in the cup
burns its holes and stokes the fire.
Star-crossed run off at the mouth job suicide;
career in the bin and bills on the mantle.
Noxious hurry cellphone distraction —
One hundred ten miles among boroughs in a tight necktie.
Hands around handles, a projector, a laser pointer
to outline the exploit and burn the
profit image on jaded eyes.
Can we truly shelter the defector
from this country within a country
at the trough, on his knees, either sucking up
or giving in?
Bell is rung and the faithful follow.
Escalator runs its mighty teeth
into the mouth of the no. 9
that echoes down the tunnel.

#7

Everyone's a lawyer or knows one.
Everyone's eating pretentious canapés
and sipping Chardonnay at happy hour.
Everyone's looking over everyone's shoulder
and everyone's *"pardon me"* is sincere.
Everyone has a portfolio of one kind or another
and everyone's work has the sheen of tempered chocolate.
Everyone's got the newest thing;
everyone's hip is either ringing or beeping or both.
Everyone's being hip to everyone else's schtick
and everyone's doing their best lap dance for the boss.
Everyone's being watched and everyone's voice mail
is being tapped.
Everyone's password is *Zeus* and everyone's playing
for the part, to be tapped for the job the next guy up
just got booted from.

#8

You are the Great Pretender; swagger of unearned bravado
pretention swathed with a forked-tongue bull-rush of deception.
Late-thirties married svengali rocking a retarded cradle.
Take your crass, divisive aggression
your skanky, coke-fiend slut-puppet secretary
your sophomoric, poorly-informed corporate drivel
your 24/7 arrogant cellphone ego-posture
your box of stale donuts and self-hating jew platitudes and go fuck yourself.
Arcane memos blindside the Blackberry with beaucoup attachments.
You pull the wool down over the innocent eyes of management
            and slither away like a snake gorged on a rat.
Fuck you and the white Benz you rode in on.
Black Jaguar pounces into traffic and klaxon.
Your past follows you like a crystal ball and chain
that foresees the inevitable reptilian brain regression.
Crawl back into your dark hole where no one can see
the fateful gaze of your hidden pain!

*How do you titillate an Ocelot? Oscillate its tits a lot.

Crack the World

Crack old Babylonian rock code; DaVinci mystery rebate in chaos.
Basilisk magenta-eyed fire glow in the distance poisoned the Nile
as Alexandria burned with all proof of the Magdalene in France.
Libraries burned and left a crack in history.
King of Serpents, snake monster in the Chamber of Secrets
is born from a chicken egg, hatched beneath a toad
and all who are fixed with the beam of its eye
shall suffer instant death.
It flees only from the crowing of the rooster, which is fatal to it.
Crack the dim lit world in which he slithers.
Crack the misfit world —
World of homeless vitamin-deficient conspiracy peddlers;
world of golden snake-oil ambush crackhead cartoon characters
mugging cornbelt daughters visiting Broadway
or on horse-drawn combines at weekend line dances.

Crack the world that pipes its backbreaking rhetoric
through universal muzak catastrophe!
Crack the book in flames and suck the words back in again.
Extinguish this persistent little speck that I am, crack this iota, this mere
rumination; sparkle in the eye of my immigrant father, off the boat into lush-life
midtown garment center, coca alencon cannabis lace paisley psychedelic.

Crack this commuter train in half and see me, head thrown back
New York Post crossword splayed, half-done in a dusty lap.
The trains in Spain lay mainly on the plain these days —
Crack that 3/11 train bomber's diabolical brain! Plastique his icy mustache!
Switch tracks to the line that rumbles Kerouac's ghostly head on
bales of old beat-hay!

Gap grows wider in silent elevator throng —
I am falling through the cracks, wasted beyond recognition.
My parts are flung wider than robot Osiris!
I won't be composed any longer; I can only drag this longing into flames
melt and rebuild.

Crack it right through your pretzel dust lapel, your proud trailer park machinery.
Grind like molars on a pork rind, through endless Oscar Meyer.
Rosy 40th St. buyer taunts a thousand sellers into giving up their failed careers
for a future on EBay "phishing" identities.

Mighty mommy magnet special carcass sniffer Labrador bogs the hunt with affection.
Shotgun cracks through duck thorax.
Dark blood drools on wicker bird-trap.

Crack the ambiguous world where governments are stolen in broad daylight
under the stuffed noses of Supreme Court justice miscarriage.
Crack the horrific world that sloughs genocidal death squads like shoulder dust.
The water rushes down
deep into a burning abyss
creates a killer tsunami
of boiling seawater — A butterfly reflex.

Tanks roll across petrified sand-glass
abuse the rights of everyone in the wrong and that's everyone.
Crack the terrorist c4 bubble-fuse.
Camels bearing arms tumble into great Sinai dune-chasms.
Sun-stroked Saudis crack thin, mad smiles at our sacrifice.
N. Korea cracks angry atoms as shields against imperial US bullet-coin.
Pope cracked the pearly gates and found no one home
no sheep and no shepherd, only mountains of bones.

Gut a sacred lamb and make an offering to this angry god
this wrathful, merciful, imaginary, mercenary, wrong god.
Butterflied and splayed, running bloody god.
Armless and legless, mute, maimed and paralyzed god.
Phantom miracle of hollow blessings; dumb and dumber god.

Crack your mind ripe open with facility
to hide the terror; mask the mud
with a malted, muzzle the broken child with Muppets.
With a hole in your face, eyes vacant and resigned you
mark pretentious misanthropes with madness unjustly
only to become the penultimate host
next to last to introduce
the final poet/prophet that sings a lore and legend
from beyond the universe, our own blood history
most accomplished by virtue of most pain endured.

Crack your mind that hides what it feels
and suffers in silence to abide by parameters
that neither nourish or mend but fester in old wounds
denying what's needed to heal.
Crack open the hiding place, flatten all eggshells.

Don't simply co-exist — Level the playing field
display every single quirk.
Backed into a corner, liable for a fraud
the great hysterical masquerade —
    Crack open the world
    make it resonate.
You may fall between the tracks
but remain revealed
and don't be a slave.

Crack the world's panic attack with mass gas-x-tra-venous media blitz.
Crack the morbid code, cellphone to hip, catch you after my next meeting crap.
Crack the world's dense membrane, a fine drip brew of bad news and
venti latte nausea.

Break the Catholic stronghold, Jewish guilt trip, Muslim *fatwa*
from scarring another bigot-blind generation.
Crack the catechismal approximation of salvation
like egg over the papal crown.
Who knows what goes on behind the scenes, in the wings?
Who knows what really goes down?
You know what you know because you told yourself so
through all the things you repeat.
You need to break the habit, crack that pattern.
There's nothing to be gained from cheap theatrics.
Crack the mind-vise driving history cross-eyed.
Crack the general gene panic; track every phantom stem cell
every CRISPR SKIP to my Lou my darling.
Break the back of the raging bull with science.

II

I need a breakthrough, need to break through the muck and mire
of materialism —
Need to break open the box, weave a new thread;
string a new fantasm balloon kite above my gate.
Crack the cannibal soup pot before I'm cooked.
Gotta break that camel's back
or I'm gonna bust a gut
and there won't be any divine sympathy.
If you break bread with enemies, they spread a poison butter.

Scientists sit around a deep concrete basement
legs and wrists shackled to wooden chairs
yellow-highlight death formulas, drunken tragedies
obscure intoxicant cosmic justice.

Burning smoke stinks of venomous crude from
deep dwindling cracks in the desert where the evidence
remains at odds with what we're fed.

Stars and stripes overhead boom in one voice
        steal stars from cold desert skies.
Please tell me who is fighting who.

All sides lose — Everything dies.

> *"…and you shall bind them for a sign upon thy hand*
> *and they shall be as frontlets between thine eyes."*

Look through the cracks at what's left.
Peek through holes in the armor.
See past the next disaster; next rosy glass shattered
next election charade.
Cracked chad changes everything
and the world is cracked.
The world is cracked
and can't be patched up.
We will never be whole until we
market the ironic antidote, broadcast sanity
spool nation's borders into gold thread
to close all wounds
merge all parties
yoke all evens and odds into one.
Fill the cracks and repave a road home
teach our kids to ride it where it goes.

Atomic Psalm

Heard by teeming masses
vaporized in pure white-hot roar of
Celestial Lion casting a star off its mane
down into our barren desert to burn;
a straw parallax zoomed down to a mushroom cloud.

Heard in the café of a small depressed town
stripped of its storefronts
by Walmart marching on

left with only boarded up adits to flop tenements
where the desolate ponder their millennial dilemma.

Heard as a piton in the rock, caliper to the brake
deep diver in the bay stirring up a bed of mud
to sling at the father, son and ghost.

Heard without regret, without hope, with only
shuddering evanescence of bright white light
in the morning of endless voice mail, junk emails from
endless listserves; digital banners wave another
1024 two cent click-throughs to the divine URL
flashing bloodshot links to heaven.

Heard as a single booming voice to
announce the end of an age —
Muslim carpet store displays new design from Beirut;
a finely detailed rug of hovering helicopters and crossed Uzis.

The pain of addled immune systems reach through
the mirror of some future medicine cabinet to grasp
a phial of antidote.
Cramped calf presses the clutch a thousand times
to inch down the interstate and end the day's
harsh commute.

God sheds grace in a warm dark stream.
God sheds grace so suffering has meaning.
School bus driver puts on his flak jacket.
Purple mountains strip mine bleeds rust down Main St.

God sheds grace on the little bomb that could.
God sheds grace on their ashen outlines on charred stone.
God sheds grace like an immortal coil
    that would heal this burning wound.

Sing above the din of a century's screams and rage.
Sing once and for all that we will not be deafened, blinded or afraid.
    Our song heard as we open the door
    to the next thousand years on Earth.
    Our blue ball fades into vast distance of space.

As we open the universe of cell
and walk up the spiraled path of spliced genes apotheosis
    blood thickens with nanobots linked to neural net
    whatever the named range of city's grid —
Taxis dart like fish to the dark spots
emerge into brilliant daylight of the end time.

HR

The month I waited in limbo
for the College Board's decision to
go with the other guy
was a hell that I conscribe
on HR and their heirs
for a hundred generations.
Silent smiles can't assuage a candidate's anxiety faced
with the unemployment line.

Everything is secret. Everything is lies.
Nothing about you can be truly known
until they mine your social profiles
and uncover your subtle regrets, kinks and bias.

The science of people in transition is neither soft nor exact
driven by fear of hunger, isolation and death.
You can't have a family without a job
whether it's Director of Corporate Development or a Taxi hack.

So Subhash, Manu, Jaya, Rajiv, Vijay, Nooshin and Mrinal; my friends
in the 'order of the curried recruiter';
my rate cannot fall below $55 an hour, that's my nut
what I need to pay my bills, dude.
I reject the low balls you recently threw...
        ...What? I am having trouble understanding you —

Barnes & Noble reposted the job with a lower salary cap
and strung me along for weeks while they interviewed
cheaper and hungrier 'ops' guys from whom they
ultimately chose.

There to mediate the most strained relations between peers and reports;
the occasional Monday morning projectile vomiting in the men's room or
late-night back office coke snort to meet a deadline in shorter order than not.
There's no length to which they will not go; no burden they will refuse to bear
unless of course it's really easy to get away with being a superficial hardass
sonofabitch and then all bets are off.

Suck ass with a smile they always say
to make sure you can thumb your nose and take crap under fire.

Why? Because money is by its nature unreasonable
but fear is not and without coin
things can get pretty dire; they don't care you got a 5 year old.

The merry PHR and his family out for a day on the lake.
Sorry, the general store is closed, you'll have to dig your bait yrself.
Should be easy to find some worms, like attracts like —
He arranges them in moss like his own consulting firm.

"Yeah, I'll get back to you by Friday" he said at least seven times
but never got back to me. Pompous V.P. turned his back
as I left the interview during which he failed to impress me
drew an org chart and put me on the spot to name three stages of the SDLC
as it relates to SOX compliance.
I am no programmer or security analyst Joe and you're so safe being aggressive
strangled by your own protocols and extraordinary results on the backs of others.
My reference was no help and no one knew how you did it
so they take your shit as fast as you deal it.

*

Now, a self-employed consultant on a long-term engagement
with PwC's global marketing and sales team.
I'm in the lion's den, on the spot, in the spotlight.
I make strategic calls under stress; run six Webex meetings before 5
pass the presentation ball, juggle two laptops and forty screens
invoice my time, fight back fatigue
with Flavia espresso and dark chocolate covered almonds.

Tomorrow, maybe I'll be a digital file clerk, a hand-sewer, an Ebola nurse
a banjo player, an Enterprise Architect —
Tackle a tomato puree with eleven cloves of my own garlic
a cup of wine, a handful of herbs, palm of salt, seven grinds —
All HR needs to do is stand there like the porcelain dolls they are.

After that, I'll be a trance channel, music pirate on a cannabis ship.
I'll get a license, grow a business like a sticky web, a sail to
catch winds of desire and hunger; crispest taco shells & carnitas —
You will not realize how much time has passed
in your stony food truck on the mountain pass above Boulder.

It's just your struggle with title and identity;
you let them tell you who you are, name you.

Unexpected car expenses and bourbon-soaked self-pity feed the rage
a demon on your back with all hopes to avoid
any face to face with HR that can be saved.
Mask cracks and spills your liquefied thorax into the
space of the interview.

*

“So, who are you?” Nonplussed red pencil notes and checkmarks fly.
She checks email from the very most corner of her eye;
partially listening for slight limitations, relative spark
about-faces and on the fences and overt fears
stoic restraint of tears or smiles and stares that avert contact.

Never ever react, ever, to anything. Does she know I’m a stoner?
Blow a silent kiss to get on her astral good side
draw a Reiki power symbol above her head descending.
Download the solution, the key to what she lost
anything to let me win the toss this time.

Eleven resumes out today. Will HR respond?
I max around six replies per month but sometimes the machine fills up.
Maybe more torture or a real step forward — Who knows?
Inbox, inbox what do you see? Will it be feast or famine for me?

*

Grasping at editorial pencil straws in a forest of bamboo fingernail shunts
and upward exacto knives in a smurf cup, resource allocations indicate a shortfall.
User Acceptance Testing is rejected; no one wants any more new technology.
No one wants a new platform; no one wants ultra-efficiency.
No one needs a new agency; no one bleats at a fresh posting.
No one clamors for a Skype interview with a Belgian cloud software company.
No one wants the fucking interview OK!?
No one has a good balance of technical and creative skills.
No one will accept the terms set to sell his soul and take the ‘blue’ pill.
No one will relocate to Atlanta or south Jersey to manage a project.
No one will walk with you to Grand Central talking shop and dodging junkies.
No one is pressing C2; no one is making their fourth double-espresso at 5PM.
No one can believe the great rate you’re getting or the 56 hours you put in last week.
No one is 55 and totally sick and tired of this shit frankly.
No one has missed their daughter’s childhood.
No one has no deep bonds, no real friends, serious debt.

No one can't play a single song by heart anymore.
No one can recite last quarter's numbers by rote though.
No one has seventy-two browsers open.
No one is pioneering his very own new stress cancer.
No one is exasperated by ferociously driven consultants
who won't take no for an answer.
No one is placating 108 other demons who know nothing of what they speak.
No one had a two hour commute in sleet and fog sheets.
No one did New York Post Tuesday crossword in fourteen minutes.
No one sobs when the database corrupts.
No one blacks out in motion and careens off a quantum track.
No one walks an implementation roadmap plank or updates a comms plan for two.
No one spends Saturday sparring with car salesmen.
No one just wants a fair deal and no bullshit.
No one prickles and swears when deceived.
No one is lost and wanders in *Laniakea Jambudvipa* false paradise writhing in
existential agony and a heavy backpack.
No one just got a pink Freudian slip.
No one is searching for the invisible gateway.
No one is just so goddamn bone-tired of being hit by the cosmic mallet over and over.
No one can't hide it anymore and is totally WYSIWYG and trigger-happy.
No one is overworked and underappreciated big time; big deal.
No one reads quietly at 2AM and awaits the new job postings.
No one watches way too many Alaska bush reality shows and imagines he's
taking down a Caribou in the conference room.

*

When it's all about hours, what you put in, when and how detailed each entry you lose perspective on the journey. Peerage and entitlement is skewed by authority not intelligence, hunger not compassion, manager tied and bound by policy, not morals. A performance review can only reveal so much and then you must rely on discreet monitoring. Whose butt best covered is a bit tainted and contrived but pucker up anyway and survive.

Anguished calendar glance, not enough hours, too many bills; all those dollars tick by and collapse into a heap of digital Harvest stubs. Not enough hot tubs and back rubs to trim the pissed-off angst from the oft-neglected reply as regards my status. I line my candidate magnet box with lead, bitter melon my BBQ sauce for a long commute, lemon rind the phone receiver and gloss over what's next with what you wish would be; Italian sesame cookies, macarons and tea, an empty agenda and seven seas.

Poems Written At Work While I Should Have Been Working

1

This banana on my desk
is now one conference call
overripe
and that sassy V.P. of Process Improvement
has made my skin crawl for the fourth time today.
I slump beneath my chair, swiveled away
from all pertinence.

I once went by "Fake it till you make it."
Now I just fake it
and make my umpteenth resolution
to break this chain, wearing thin;
check-off my final action item:
the removal of this mask I've lived in.

2

An unreported quagmire lays in wait with
a hash of paper branches overlayed to
camouflage the pothole from the help desk.
Slathered in anti-chafing gel and heat dope, smoking soldering guns spin
by their trigger guards, slip into leather holsters
like a cellphone.
The square-jawed latin technician with three names avers a superior tone
as he attempts to plug a 20 amp plug into a 30 amp receptacle.
Late hours cannot stave off the next eventual debacle.

Rapid clicks obfuscate the database of database logs.
Screen after screen, field upon field, pop-downs
pop-ups, call-outs strobe in strained rapid eye movement
to mimic my waking nightmare
that involves a Javascript harpy, Hekyll & Jekyll, a drooling XML ogre
six security gnomes, a dominatrix receptionist
and a flatulent fortune teller before a crystal ball plasma screen as dark as onyx.
These forecasts as unpredictable as trees next to fall;
all circle the same swirling newmedia metadata drain
and clawing out of each catalytic digital breath, a tear, screech of tires, call for help.

3

It's a very thin dime to stop on
rarified air at the peak of Mt. 'Contention'
in a strong gust to shake your already tenuous footing
on the tech cliff of the day
challenge your memories retention
of every position gone from bad to worse in a flash
of poor decisions and impossible circumstance
realized when errors become disasters and
disaster recovery fails to recover
those dull gems of sales and dusty client profiles
that roll over and die with the chance slip of a magnet.

Another job honeymoon is over before it began
as the buzz of a resume fades on the front lines
in the face of shrapnel flung
by an exploding business case
and the blood of we lambs that wet the
manicured paws of lions
in a gratis buffet feast.

4

I wish I cared. I wish I didn't care so much.
I am mostly scared of being one of those victims
whose boss causes him a stroke or heart attack at work.
I would die because I cared too much.
When I don't care, it's easier;
easier to take the blame, play the endless political games
let the chips fall where they may —
Easier to let the customer wait, or go elsewhere;
easier to watch the axe fall, sour grape gumdrops for all
easier to keep down my bologna on a hard roll
when I just don't care
but this scares me more than being broke
than losing my house, my wife, kids, books, smoke, sanity —
This puts me out and makes me hate my career
which it really isn't anyway.

5

Hunger vanishes in the wake of a glazed donut
slid down my throat late morning after Thanksgiving holiday.
By 1PM I imagine a burger
to fill my belly and some time on this sore Monday
until 5PM comes and I drop my mask and
run for the door;
sweep every issue and task under the rug
and hustle my buns home
to take my place on the sofa
and release my mind in peace for a few hours
until the sweet shipwreck of sleep erases
all vestige of concern. Dawn again returns
to slice apart my dreams and
burn down what routes of escape I'd built;
locks of a canal drained dry as I pass through
the narrow channel, in a single direction
out to sea, gone in search of home, adrift in crossed winds
that leave no trace of how they go.

6

Washed down four Tramadol with Dunkin Donuts brew
and wait for the edge to be cut
for my back and knee I threw out cutting trees
to float in that faux opiate glow
so I can map out a whole new order processing workflow in Visio
and bounce that old mail server running OS 10.2 (Puma).

Abraded leather notebook, worn thin as my neck skin
from rubbing and sighing, rubbing and sighing
in meeting after meeting after meeting
while a fire alarm like a cuckoo drives the lobby crazy.
No smoke, only winter sun glare through venetian blinds.
Hazy bar charts point to outdated crimes
of putting the consumer last and the
fleet of tarnished parachutes first.

Run, run for your lives down Rt. 503 toward Moonachie!
Run, run for your lives!

7

You watch me with gears turning hard
behind jaded eyes, judging my appraisals
and apologies with backhanded suspicion.
Why should I apologize for not being able to pull
the CGI rabbit out of a web server's hat
or intuit which packet was dropped at the switch?
When you don't know what's wrong
you blame the guy that tries to fix it until it's fixed
then you move on without a thank you
and pretend to be ticked off that it took so long.
This is why I am writing while I should be working
to take a stand on myself, who I really am;
while inclusive, cannot be persuaded to bend
cannot be broken, cannot be pushed and shoved into quicksand
or lost forever in menial tasks
that keep the wool pulled down
over these varicose bearings that were once my eyes
that now jump and jitter in the dark
to try and see who may be watching
as I navigate high seas in a paper boat
to earn the right to land.

8

Conference call antics accelerate in recession;
a group circle jerk by remote.
Hairy palms in Springfield, Indianapolis, Williamsburg, Louisville
smoke from the heavy friction
in mutual deflection
to ignore heads that roll by across the killing floor.

Market sunk to low not seen since my first divorce.
Pink slips fly in West Side Hwy winter sun glare.
That same jerk in blue BMW cut me off recklessly as usual.
He probably runs some major corporation about to ruin a thousand fools
like me and you who didn't get out in time;
got stuck defending their seniority and now have only their 401k
to be hit with a stiff penalty once they straighten up and
button their pants.

Face the most monumental shitstorm yet —
21st century depression now sporting the most phenomenal
soup kitchen sign in sparkling car wash chrome spinners and buzzing neon.

Call enters its second hour and the drone weakens briefly
as I yawn and ponder unreasonable gratitude, sourceless, causeless, and wan.

9

I'd rather be fingerpainting with hot encaustic on shards of sharp glass.
I'd prefer to be a lone duck on a slick of spilt oil
        spiraling into a dark eddy.
I'd 'druther' to dream I was lost in a huge automat
        without a single coin.
I'd rather make a scene at a sleepy PTA meeting
        demanding the removal of a motorized nativity scene
        that won't let me sleep.
I'd prefer to be dipped in gasoline and sent blindfolded into
        an AC/DC concert during the wait for the encore
        5000 Bics flicked and flying high.
I'd be better to be besotted by swine and tormented by
        flat-chested asian schoolgirls
or be trampled by holiday Walmart shoppers grabbing rayon nighties
or whet against the sidewalk like a sharp popsickle stick knife
or mauled by minke whales in an aquarium mishap
or be picked on by mean Eddie Vedder like Jeremy.

I've said my last today.
If it were only my last day today
I would walk out into the frozen parking lot, my breath a sour steam.

10

Dream job vanished in a cold morning commute.
Stomach churns on Dunkin glazed stick and my boss, Duncan
arrives from Nashville with a monumental chip
on his shoulder, smell of burning mustache hair.
Dream become a nightmare, my brain is on fire
and frost is on the sinister pumpkin that missed its chance
to be a dark, overcooked pie for a bonusless holiday.
"Who, if I cried, would hear me among the angel's executive committee?"

My dream has died again today in that I am just too goddamn tired
of it all to remain asleep
so I somnambulate through the day
and sublimate my grief —
Lay myself down to dream of finally dreaming;
take my seat at an empty table
before an empty glass
a drop of quicksilver.

11

You can hide in moonlight but you can't run from shadows.
You can dish it but you can't get it on the spoon.
You can be hung out to dry, hardly able to breathe.
You can get paid but the piper won't be satisfied.
You can try to sharpen your blade but the edge dulls too easily.
All these clichés and more in your inbox before noon.

You can do a lunchtime crossword in the cafeteria but not at your desk go figure.
You can clean up the server room but not be able to find a highlighter or a cable tie.
You can bide your time but never abide;
crack your own ceiling but never attain the dream of retirement.
Ride the 2% annual raise tide but never arrive poolside.
Drink your wine but never feel it.

Purge caches, purge zucchini sticks, purge bad vibe database vendor.
Bring the old Macs back up, lead the Dells out to pasture.
Get out from under the bus, go on, get up.
You can get behind a mountain but you may never move it.
You can strap on a titanium truss but this shit is just too fucking heavy.
You better make it look good even if it sucks.

12

Surely it is love that sustains me
yet a mighty wind could lift my heart up
far above this treacherous tumult
and free me to a new wonder;
i.e., a cash windfall or the megamillions lottery
an Amazon.com marketplace or EBay score, my own web empire jewelry store.
That and love would sustain me just a bit more

as if all my years of toil and trouble earned me something
other than just a paycheck. Still, I am grateful not to be
rummaging dumpsters in mall parking lots yet
or waiting in an endless queue for a cold loaf of survival
to hold me up like a walking stick.
She hands me a talking stick that gives me the floor
validates my voice, places my next bet

and she is as soft as the economy
and she dances on a lotus flower in my chest
and she practices peace, an anomaly among beasts
that play at humanity in hopes we might one day achieve it.

Surely she sustains me
and walks the finest line beside me
hot razor's edge that keeps all five eyes wide open.

13

It could all be much worse.
I could be a deckhand on one of those 'dangerous' fishing boats
being thrown across the rail by a frozen wave.
I could still be cooking toast, cutting out rounds, pouring
bad gravy on them to make stage prop 'medallions of beef' for underachievers
playing *"The Importance of Being Earnest".*
I could be entirely delusional and not just mildly oblivious.
I could need a handful of Xanax to get out my door.
I could insult my boss and ruin our tenuous rapport.
I could be hit with an ancient curse that turns my sweat to acid
and burns me as I work.
It could all be much, much worse;
fall off a chair alone like Michael Corleone, dead and alone
a sole dog barking.
No one to call me at 10AM, say *"I love you, hang in there it'll all be OK, don't worry."*

I could have a boss who actually sits directly behind me, watching my every move
barking critical directions, maneuvers of the persnickety
promoted to 'protocols of strategic idiocy'
and then, on top of it all, your expense check could bounce.
Your cat could hide your flash thumb drive with the presentation
you worked on all weekend.
You could just be old and tired but with NO talent

and then you'll really be up the creek without a paddle;
without a lens to focus, without any better options
without a friend, without the mind to make amends.
Migraines from dawn to dusk
and no tap to drain the temple's sturm & drang
so it clogs up a vein and throbs like a red tusk.
Impaler of peace and gray threads an afterthought
for the beast, rushed by taxi to make the boardroom
rubber chicken, rice & beans, tricyclic martini drowse.

Stale reports bantered like real news;
chart like a spider alit upon his tuffet, a prehistoric mastodon in business color.
Old news is a weak gorilla unable to grasp a branch to swing down
so it falls amid rotted leaves and crumbles like a wet log on the loading dock
cracking heavy with ice which will leave no evidence.

14

Rack of servers beneath a new power drop
balks at being my savior
walks a thin line of marginal usefulness
wracks my brain with irrelevant details
a burger slider, Drakes Coffee Cake.
Steel snake through hung ceiling sounds like
a wooden frog w/ ribbed back
pulled up and through, zipping 30 Amps to my next headache.
401K loss brings a dismal rollover.
Traffic routing graph tells me nothing;
the weak link in the net wears a cloak of invisibility.

On my cell for 2 ½ hours with HP.
The back room smells like glue and old ink
an inch of dust on concrete.
Eighteen updates and reboots later
there is still a huge gap as large as
the Sea of Tranquility.

15

A rainy Wednesday in January —
Eyelid twitch calmed via spinal twist

like crack of a dozen whips at once.
In Jersey, pay to play Ponzi politicians pray to not get caught
slide 20M into an offshore account
while mom and pop liquidate their asses to eat
and keep a roof hung overhead as the storm rages.

Missiles fly over bloody desert
and children cry, orphaned and abandoned.
Bread, a shingle, hard tack grit with a crude schmear
lost in a 2-ton mushroom 'poof'.

My baby's heartbeat is strong, coming in for final approach.
Obama takes over the White House, warns against depression.
Where was he twenty years ago when I was really depressed?
I am warned by an inverted nipple
oozing fresh white pearls of milk.
I am warned by sun glare on the Garden State
and errant, barreling Fed-X trucks.
I am warned by a Gigabit Ethernet network sensor
that traffic has peaked and I cannot work.
I am warned by slap-happy lotterists that
the Mega-ball odds are 75 million to one.

16

Heroic shiver puts hair on end
driving down Rt. 17 frigid commute.
Start the week strong and salted
new shirt crisp and as blue
as my horoscope makes me
with assurances of a turnaround.

When a man's world falls apart
and loss creates an emptiness to fill
over decades of heartache
he would much rather take a bitter pill
than open to that pain for pain's sake.

A job is just a job
but it tears your heart out
and leaves you weary and spent
wondering where the years went

and missing everyone that has passed
all by no fault of their own
only life, by nature always leaving us
left to shoulder the ongoing sorrow
and small pieces of dreams remembered.

17

A purple heart gleams on dark Navy blue lapel.
It kicks blue blood like a baby in the womb
pushes out from darkness toward the playing field.
All god's children lock and load in the rising gloom of dawn
take their seats in the real class for the real lessons
in how to claw one's way up the rungs of success.

Twisted smile hides apprehensive trust.
Taunt and torment by sideways glance talking fast about
what you must know to survive.
A rack full of wood, a few chickens, a roof, a stash is not enough
to keep your boots tied tight
keep your bowl filled with rice
keep your skin thick and tough.
It won't suffice to clamber and strive;
let down your aching guard and be at ease.
To get dreams realized
by war and sword alone, keys need
to be filed to fit a moving target —
Open a door, close one, and forget about it.

18

Bored beyond belief by her slithering monotone
Pam, the corporate witch parks her broom by the door
and shakes black dust all over the fancy marble floor
drapes her cape with pointy hood over a groaning chair.

Verify, validate, vett it out; get on the same page, get yr crones in a row.
Get on board with my numbers, get with the program; get your Powerpoint
act together, get it straight, get on it, get your black magic show on the road.
Get bored with it, get hot crazy bored, lock, stock and BINGO board bored;
bite your fingernails to the quick bored, lay down for elective waterboarding bored
beat me with a locust stick bored, bite my lip and swallow it bored

bored to the core, bored to a loud snore;
bored of "IT", Information Technology that complicates everything
even things that are very simple.
Get my message, get the flock out of here;
get approximate, get 'Appomattox to Beauregard'.
Get the encyclopedia, get me a drink, get me drunk on Jack then get me a cab.
Get a kick in the pants for no reason, get hip to the real reason, get the job done.
Get over yourself.

19

Am I a good person?
Do I deserve success and happiness?
Am I afraid of this pen?
Muse shoots through the ink, a wire transfer
from a point beyond infinity; filtered sun zips
across a tilted chrome shaft like a message.
Fear shoots down my throat like a noose
that winds a fatal loop

and still I have got to ask ... Am I a good man?
Could the sum of my resistance earn me a star
or am I fated to run myself into the ground
before I lay down;
cry my throat raw
over what I don't have
and what I can't do?

Life and death is everywhere
and at every place within me.
Here I am — I am dying.
Here again — I'm alive.

The poison of ego is tasty
but goes down hard.

20

The sum of all intent
leads you to this moment
to either rant and vent against the phantom corporate moloch
or be the antidote, the lotus in mud

hub of the wheel that drives an elusive satisfaction
of a job well done; money made and in the bank
a shot of Jack and a big rib-eye steak.

Stuck in the midst of a war between V.P.s
I take the fall, I am the fall guy — Fell on my digital sword
to make a point; you can't put a diamond into
a cardboard setting, you will lose it.

The sum of all regret
is a sloshing cup of joe
that might motivate or slow you down
depending upon how you carry the cup, how you sip.
Take your eyes off the road for even a fleeting moment
and risk an impact, a crash into the truck ahead.
A detested colleague hanging by a thread
that becomes a noose —
Career suicide being fashionably 'In'
among those whose talk is far bolder
than their walk;
whose neck is stuck out farthest
dark axe poised to sever their head.

21

Abort — Abort — Danger: Network slowness ahead.

Pray for a simpler life; less stress, more pleasure.
The veil is paper thin, a wisp —
Planets shift, solar winds change direction
ball of *karma* bounces wildly;
one day bogged in dark results
the next bursting with light, kiss on a valentine.
Again and again I press the same button
hope for a different result; I must be insane.

Support is illusory and once you get used to the free fall
you can start to look around a bit, have a bit of fun
before you hit the ground.

Mind queue length bottlenecks on itself
as prayers go nowhere but out there.

22

At this point my memory is dubious
and the only chips I've got are on my shoulder.
My nails are in a heap of shards on my desk
in a litter of crumbcake and crumpled sticky notes.

Sore hand, sore chest, sore leg, sore heart
from tumbling down the road after my Dyna Wide-Glide.
Hit a horny deer head on
          running blindly to catch his doe
          caught a cop's bullet instead
          and then another.

In my chair in a daze of hydrocodone
the sickly sweet smell of Dolores's musk
wafts down the hall — I can't run
and it overtakes me. I gag and sip my coke
hold my breath to let the musk tsunami pass.
Sore head, sore nose, sore eyes, sore feet
beat the pavement like a tribal drum
and forget everything I've become.

My 'sort of' colleagues pass my door and think
I am writing notes regarding the latest security hole.
Nope, just a poem, a place to pour my fading dreams
like flat beer into a Dixie cup.

To bring the bacon to the table
I carry on the best I'm able
and write what few words I can between
workday hassles and baby bottles, squeaky doors and countless chores.
Totally slammed from dawn to dusk
and left no room for a poet's repose
to contemplate the universe, a rose.

23

An innocent, concerned question by a gay Chinese archivist
is an invitation to vent and rant about everything that's wrong
every slight imposed, every transparent effort to toss me under a bus
or is it?

Back at it — I re-imaged and configured a Windows 2003 server
sent out a few resumes, mailed a nasty certified letter to Sleepy's
re: their defective box spring and "Madoff-like" scam of the
retail bedding industry — How do *they* sleep at night?

Why do we work so hard and pretend to enjoy it?
It's a tortuous, tenuous life; a hurried, hassled hell.
So much loss, death, pain inflicted and endured.
I am ashamed to be human more often than I care to tell
or admit — Chills go up my back in quiet moments.
Not even a daily pop of Prozac can relieve my anxiety;
my fear is a hard crust of cradle cap
on my soul's infant head.

I pray for each day to be done quickly — Run to the exit
speed down the highway — Fear ripple temporarily abates
a shimmer long enough to reflect my face
and what do I see?

A promise unfulfilled.

24

Squeaky Fromme is being released after thirty-four years in jail
and I'm still here at my desk
biting my fingernails to the quick
on another painfully slow day.
Sound of a box fan drones.
I checked CNN.com eighty-three times so far
and still have no idea what's going on.

Sharks become weakfish, darts become feathers.
Evil eye softens into sultry lash bats and twinkle.
Deranged murderers become matronly holy rollers
released to preach weeks before their death
about their hard-won reformation
replete with tongue-tied gospel flubs through stage pancake
so thick their faces craze like sugar glass in an ice storm.

Soldiers come home from Afghanistan
with PTSD bad like a jittery eye twitch and
feverish 'what's the point?' morose bug, a desert tan

souvenir can of C-Rations and a limp dipstick.
Here I am still at my desk
worried about CGI errors, strange 'pathpings' and
ugly web pages misbehaving with IIS.

25

Momma gets a "Me" day.
Baby Jesse poops twice to our great delight.
Office is slow as molasses running uphill in January.
I'm having a "You" day
trying to pick my fights;
the ones I can win —
Spray chlorothalonil on my tomatoes
to fight "Late Blight"
bite the hand that feeds me a bitter pill.
Rise & shine, put on your suit and tie
sit down at your desk and die.

Momma's getting dentures.
Baby Jesse's yet to get her first bottom two.
I still can't chew ice cream
nor stomach convention.
I'm looking for a "Me" day too.
Looking for a "Me" week —
Looking for a couple of "Me" years in a row
where I can sleep until I wake
eat until I'm sated
and get down to the real work
fulfill what I know is true
drive my sword into a glazed ploughshare
and write about "You"
your day in the grand adventure
land of milk & honey & antivirals.

26

To sign how I feel about driving Rt. 17
I would flip you a large bird and mean it.
At least 1/3 of all commuters are idiots, half asleep;
weave in and out of congested lanes with inches to spare

talk on their cellphones or primp their hair
try to get home seconds before you do
so they can sit in a chair and stare at the tube.

It's an inane, insane, outrageous, outlandish
out and out crazy, fast push to nowhere.
Hyper-aggressive suicidal road rage
to get to jobs we ultimately hate;
to get home and put our families through equivalent torture
to make our egos feel better, share the pain
secretly drowned in liquor or six scoop sundaes.

High heels slowly clip-clop across linoleum
like tired mares marching toward the gluc jar.
I slip out at 4:45PM through the roar of the air conditioner
that blows across my servers.

> Data is best served cold
> but too much knowledge is hell
> when it lies unused.

27

Tigers become kittens
harpys become bluebirds
grovelers become CEOs.
Mindfuckers become slurring dumb bunnies after 5PM
simpering little rodents who sniff out an orange rind, a martini olive
a bit too close to the 3AM brass rail —
Porcelain bus destination — Red Eye Blvd.

Red-faced cubicle voyeurs become white-collar inmates at Sing Sing.
Red-headed, freckled secretaries become complicit in
the mass embarrassment, your nameplate on the door
covered over by a laser printed sign "Someone Who Doesn't Listen".
Manager with the handlebar mustache getting a bit too close
with his tirade of spittle.

Big-ass V.P. who mangled your project
becomes an out of work big-ass V.P. on a flight back to VA.
That big ass a bit too big for coach, begs not to be stuck
for hours on the tarmac, get sweaty, smelly and hot.

And what becomes of the righteous soldier of production?
He is handed a mouse, a thermos, a pica ruler and a
cyanide crush-pill, asked to fast on Nestle $100,000 bars
pending dispensation of his divine bonus.

Plant closed after being bled dry —
Employees writhe & twist in a cold wind
manage to shoot off a last venomous email to all.
"Enough is Enough!" they cry, and management responds
only to warn us all against forwarding the missive.

28

I am a glorious goldbrick
a spectacular slacker
a top-notch waster of company time.
I browse the net from 9 to 5
and pull six figures from the corporate unwise.

You're getting me crazy, making me nuts.
I'm wasting my life here in this ergonomic chair.
Should I be a poor unemployed poet
or a well-off corporate zombie?
I dare to include myself in my day.
I have the courage to be inclusive.

Roll the Dice, scour Monster, comb Careerbuilder
jump around Job Circle, hit HotJobs with a cautious vengeance.
Ever-seeking, always searching, my calling is calling.
My cap needs a feather.
Baby Jesse needs a new pair of shoes.
I need to shake these working-man blues by goofing off.

I am a purposeful procrastinator
a dynamic daydreamer
a stout layabout on the virtual couch.
I will balance my productivity against my true proclivity
to let mind, heart and eye wander free.

29

Small dried leaves swirl on concrete
sounds like windy pachinko
or shushing skis.
Fall ushers in a weak busy season
brings the freelance pool to their knees.
They beg for more hours to make their nut
pink slip like a punch in the gut.
I am so tired I can hardly say so.

I strike a diligent pose and proceed to space out entirely
so if anyone walks in I will look sufficiently busy
and engaged in some inane task or another
to put money in pockets of people who don't care about me
people who cut down trees; people dreaming of reasons to
shut down facilities, people who fester in recession
build their brick and mortar bulkhead against a rising virtual wave.

Teens line Woodcock Mtn. Rd. waiting for their school bus;
half asleep drones in a row of driveways stand
like lawn ornaments or squash awaiting harvest
plucked one by one and sat on vinyl seats.
Flashing red eyes hold up traffic
young minds carried away to be herded into groups their own age
so the spectacle will not be questioned.

The brainwash continues past graduation
when the market itself presents limited options
and these limits begin to define them.
They become us and in turn their children
become them and everyone buys in.

30

Today is *Yom Kippur*
and I am at my desk diagnosing 'Stop' errors;
monitoring bandwidth utilization
because I used my floater holiday back in April
and International Paper is definitely not a Jewish company.

My sins remain unatoned like these network errors.
Why should anyone care if my dreams die or if my name
is written in the book of eternal life?

Nu, bubbala, you shouldn't be surprised
everything you think you possess must be surrendered —
If your daddy told you different it was all lies.

Filling up the oil tank is more important than poetry.
Stack the wood pile, salt for the softener, a baby gate
a case of formula, a freezer full of meat —
These outweigh my need for words so I am left
broke, sated and silent on the rising edge of the singularity.

I could beat my chest, fling a tassel or two
in hopes to quell these transgressions
and find resolution —
Then again
I will redraw the graph
to show exactly where I am
overutilized.

Transgressions

> But may I, when again I have the city's crush
> and tangled noise-skein and furor
> of its traffic wrapped around me, alone,
> may I above that thick confusion
> recall sky and the gentle mountain rim
> on which the far off plodding herd curved homeward.
>
> — Rainer Maria Rilke
> from "The Spanish Trilogy"

I

I wade through days of light
like movable night
enter them
with a carnival of rich
carnal klaxons
blaring what I think
unable to uncover
clues about who is moving
in these tight pants and sunglasses;
who steps on New York City sidewalk's
hundred billion club-footed bacteria?

Deafening din of the "world"
declares our separateness;
walking down a gritty street
in downtown summer city stew
mass tepid squalor
compartmentalizing my
contemptuously stupid boring advertising job.

At 5:58 again
no matter what the song
clockradio curdles spirit
sours mind, kills dreaming
slays the composer writing aubades
in lazy morning afterglow.

On the dawn-chilled depot platform
I resist the deep despot echo of ghost freedom deposed
barely making it through the commute, a simple refuge.

I sink deeper into my vinyl seat
on this loco-
motive with no ulterior
centrifugal express identity crisis
journalizing these petty bourgeois inconveniences
at each of the many station stops
on this transforming track.

Temporary comfort of rattling sleep can't tame fear.
Desires sublimate under flutter of lids
and you can't hear the difference
between the voices of spirit or of ego.
Inner talk blares as towns pass quickly —
Smudge of sage and tobacco resolves the blur
sated, grateful and impatient.

What matters is the reedy purr of an old cat
a clean white sheet of paper, glass of sherry;
a good night's sleep with dreams of laughter.
Deep breathing in the alpha channel with no
ruby mask or weighted slippers or Freudian slip-
stream of sweet blackness at the center of being.

Phantom's xylophone march abductions in childhood nightmare;
paper skeletons grab yr neck and armpits, you pull the covers up close.
Aliens in the elevator shift yr lymph nodes through shallow throat —
Dad speedballs with a diabetic whose wife throws his leg prosthesis
out the 19th Fl. window
while mom gets high to Leon Russell in the kitchen with her hairdresser.
Indian doctors whisper like chipmunks in a sterile forest
of disinfected linoleum, crackle their foil and bubblewraps
            pop out a superdrug which makes things worse on purpose.

These dreams feel like moving chest-out through a swarm of bees —
You violently thrash at your artful, evasive enemy
who analyzes you with surgical apparition.

Leftover dung and litter grains hang out of the cat's butt
you kiss her anyway;
crumple up a page, drain the juice glass.
On 16th St. bright morning work walk
city keels over its incendiary bed
repeats like greasy eggs on a stale roll and

I am pointing at the moon —
May my spirit be like rock.

The "Temp" life is a freelance shaft
by wealthy bosses who ruminate on the art of resource suppression
and ram it up your ass —
So there is no problem as long as you have
no problem with that
otherwise, you will french-kiss iron storm grating
tear flesh on razor spikes of office chair floor mats
travel with an attaché of grief and heartburn, a stained tie, ink spot pocket.

Get bloody carpet burns connecting ethernet transceivers under a hundred desks.
Pavement gravel embedded in shoulder and knee, tangled in a mass of localtalk.
Red rose petals sprinkled on your forehead, shower drips on frontal bone —
They will wrestle the cellular phone from your cold, rigid fist
and you will have no big idea whatsoever.

II

Sitting meditation — Not sitting —
What's the difference?
Lotus fold of knee or
mind rasp, inhalation — Filter of
auric mouth
takes and gives pains and pleasures
folded like origami on mirror;
pulsing tingle
between scrolled eyes and thighs.

All the time
I wondered who you were
because I had no idea who I was —
It was over before we knew
it was over; just when we got
a glimmer
or because of that.

Crescent moon
in crisp October twilight
cuts through blurred vision
embraces the current dilemma.

Surrender completely to falling leaves, burning in piles;
unsharp smokescreen above orange sunset at century's horizon.
Autumn brings death
as a call to practice
mindful awareness
stir static life into sweetness;
what we cling to like newborns
ripped away impersonally from the breast
like leaves from its tree by the solvent wind.

Beauty continually ripens.
It seems like roses but blushes deeper.
It just seems and traffics in the illusory.
Place the hidden marker between us
and we always move toward that boundary.
Create the hungry mouth on yourself
and it sucks only a brief moment of forgetting
like phantom nipple rising and falling with breath.
You root for the ghost and she
suckles you in dreamtime rebirth.

Autumn renews
a call to satisfy every wish;
a sleeping song
            to last the winter long
a warmth to counter
bright coldness we deny most painfully.
Deep reminder of stellar origin
siren who calls you singing from the
blackness between stars.

I stare out the window at
blur of yellow trees in
bright sun glare.
My thoughts rush ahead
to spring, out of body
on the 7:52.

There is no hour and seventeen minutes wasted.
Each trip defines what you're made of
alone or in public
as another bead is pulled along the string.
Must careful rosary the Samaya

and not transgress it.
This pious vow of comet entrails
drives its repetitive emptiness home;
curls like incense into rams horns
crushes them with huge epochal tires, great red cushions
beneath blinding afterimage red-shifts.
Icy star pizza scraped off the
cold dark roadway acclimates quickly
halting convection; her specular black lace teddy
dresses the breasts of the Milky Way.

Mala beads tap out an invisible code
to name my aspiration; invisible man shielded from
who mustn't see me, night as I am
often marvelous yet reaching closer into fear like
abundant mackerels on my spleen
nibbling away self-esteem.
A fair day follows a suffering one
as I fall asleep in the warm satin
Indian-summer breeze.

III

Gaia mother, our survival all but forgotten
betrayed daily with a kiss and a chemical
driven away with your car and your testicles.

Forget other lives, your almond eyes
persimmon juice running down your chin.

Deep memories come forward with faces hardly recognized
masks you wore light up in sequence, a museum:
    Running through bush in Rio De Janeiro
    in 1683 on the tribal stump fasting
    from wild rice and boar.
Castle Duino crashing surf, night life in Prague
distant sound of Rodin's chisel against stone.

Carthaginian goddess worshipper
gasps with spotted fever and a curse on his breath.
Innocent youth who lay on blankets of rabbit fur
listening to Simon & Garfunkle's *Bookends*
watch a votive flicker behind colored crushed glass

crackle of hempseed through dirty windows over Murray Hill rooftops.

Sad, hobbling cripple struggles
across 11th Ave. to reach the bus stop and the bus doesn't stop —
          Head bowed in ghostly shadows of florescent shelter.

Illness takes root in slums and dark alleyways of the city
while you tune your electric guitar
and fumble through the Pentatonic
in your comfy condo with two T.V.s and a full pantry.

Blind woman in front of the Helen Keller Center
hails a taxi; lost the U-ring on the harness of her seeing-eye dog
and bent at the waist, arms outstretched, calls out "Sasha! Sasha come!
Come Sasha! Sasha!!"
Even the Pakistani cabbie calls out with her while the black lab
sniffs the curb three feet away.

That lame old man who walked past you signing Reiki
was transformed at the Union Square farmer's market —
          His cane caught your pants leg
          came out from under him and fell —
For a moment he realized he didn't need it.
You acquire his limp and count your blessings.

You forget you bless others in mysterious ways and
bless yourselves, being instruments of teachings moving through life
auspiciously with blinders.

Crow pecking carrion on frosted Palisades ride home.
Family members die mile after mile, you walk a lonesome road
          toss through sleepless nights worrying.

Every night of new love includes the danger
of eighteen years of hard work commuting from a vapid suburbia
to raise a child that will betray your image and make their own way
maybe make you proud, maybe not; President, rapist, doctor or killer
surely watch you die one day and take over your world.

Remember

simple fearless embrace of wind

maskless riding endless roads, strong as you stride
past the aisle of parked cars toward the depot platform.

Remember

when the teacher fails you can only turn to Nature
not your little 'self'.
Night steeps a rich supple mead;
your damp, slippery, witchy leather cape costume ripples.
You carry armfuls of indian corn, wear the brick bandanna of city.

Remember

you were not made to lose track of yourself on these tracks;
lose face in the face of a sea of blank stares, lose right action
right livelihood, the *Paramitas*, lose the one you love to painful cigarettes
through a salesman's mask, psychic carpet mines in your office zone.
War theatre of corporate Amerika strategized void of nature:
'no eye, no ear, no nose, no tongue, no body
no mind, no appearance, no end of appearance, no old age and death
no IRA, no Keogh, no quarterly bonus, no dental, no pension
no end of old age and death, no suffering, no origin of suffering
no cessation of suffering'.
You were not meant to suffer this way
not made mean, not *made* to suffer but to be reminded.

IV

Vanguards of meditation's temporary silence
shout primordial raw closure of millennium
come back to simple easy breathing.
They took the long way home but got there
and lived for impermanence.
Cradling Zen, I sit quietly and remember them.

Pioneers hoisting sails to course new destinies
arrive in promised lands great guns blazing their grainy, immigrant film.
They took the Ellis Isle short stick and struck a staff to part the celluloid sea
standing by the West Side Hwy. to capture newly homeless men
sitting one leg, one bottle up on the cement dividers, tilted fedoras backgrounded
by a misty Hudson sunset.

Brooklyn *Padmasambhava* on his lotus-throne barstool, swirling skullcup of
ambrosia on tap, casts thunderbolts across pure-land skies to
magnetize wandering mind.
Mahakala's consort in tight lamé, sings in her anguished pleasure
one leg across his thighs in leopard skins and pumps, eyes and fangs gleaming.
Exotic dancer devours our mutual neurosis, our transgressions are bounced
at the door.

Future schools teach crash course in Scrabble by direct chemical injection of
crossword theorems solved.
Nootropic O.J. to draconian brain stem; cloned mind of *Elohim* re-heralds new age
a mega-bio-ragtime-raga, music which generates
surreal freeform holograms, atomized fragrant oils and pulse of
tuned endorphin pleasure as you recline in your vibrating nuclear Barcalounger
in 21st century quantum schismroom chomping ginseng bonbons.

How safe with a wife and kids and condo and reliable sales job
and how dead, lost to one or another unreasonable reasonableness —
Falling out at night with a bag of Fiddle-Faddle in front of *Dynasty* to fantasize
about lives that seemed even more unreasonable though richly abundant
lives that moved from scene to scene, tortuous pain, sex, revenge, elation
without ever waking up from their programmed dream.

Open rivers of faces rushing in waves of spiked, slicked, curled, flowing
freshly washed hair dancing through Beltane —
How open morning yogurt and granola
greenness of green, redness of red, smell of coffee from street carts on 5th Ave.
Open grip on my attaché, open destiny with a face veil hiding its beauty.
Early astral AM dream reveals:
< Moving too fast on a motorized skateboard down a steep and curving hill
comedian Adam Sandler dressed in a young girl's Sunday church outfit
standing on the high dive in an Olympic swim meet, a giant Crayola crayon-mobile
like the deep mine drilling rigs from *Total Recall,* rides through the grassy field
in one huge sexual insinuation. >

V

In other homes, other ringing clocktower bells peal, other skylines hold you.
Fearless *Dharma* Bridge is approached and crossed with Radiant Intellect.
Crisis and suffering keeps you crossing avenues, keeps you dancing, groomed
to truth.
Favorite watch tells time in mantra, not hours.

Your child with limbs intact, conscious compassionate demeanor of sweetness
loves you with such pure innocence and devotion that she will be a bright polished
mirror until the day you die and become one for her; being mirrored, remembered
grateful for life beyond the limits of sense, free in the moment, at home where
nothing's happening.

Sing precious incarnation with any voice that suits you; imprint the cloudy fabric
of this blue sky realm with your unique design — No talon tears it open at the heart
to get you past the Eagle's devouring eye; tortoise rising to the surface with its head
through a ring, serpents devouring surge to ouroboros.

Your lover leaves and then returns, ripples on the mountain lake converge and spread.
Who you really are becomes a taste in your mouth like an ancient fruit you cannot name
a garden you cannot tend, beliefs you can't defend, feelings you won't recall until you
turn that corner and she's there, bright eyes swirling with mischievous light.

Leave yourself behind in the time it takes
to evaporate deep releasing signal breaths
integrate everything suppressed
to your senses dilate and forgiving.
In a flash of instant remembering
with no big deal, out of nowhere
an old friend phones and then
the touch on an elbow from a Lakota wiseman
sends up smoke signals —
He observes the environment through hawk eyes.
The hawk teaches its lesson of the "Old Way" to
a field mouse by devouring it, releasing its spirit to the wind.

Nothing is lost in that warrior's love.
No memories distract his victorious beak from the kill.
No track squeal distorts the absolute
knowing where you are truly going.

I wade through days of light like movable night
push through nights of pain
like a "wind-whipped nightflame into the lamp's mantle"
like a sun ray lifting the faces of new spring flowers
on the other side of the hill.

Just Beyond Reach

The inner world is just beyond reach.
The perfect world; just beyond reach.
A peaceful world is just beyond reach.
A simple way to live; just beyond reach.
The 'other' world is ever beyond reach;
your ancestors gather at the flip of a switch
shadows present and fleeting
just beyond reach in the dark
in a strange room where we aren't sure
but sense we know each other.
Relatives beyond reach, faces turned into hints of silhouette
against electric blue
seen from the bottom of a well.
Friends and relatives in old photographs beyond reach;
dried flowers in faded sepia shadows of ancestry.

Trans-humanist cybernetic bio-integrated technologies are just beyond reach.
Affordable entertainment for the jaded — Forever beyond reach.
Endless mountain curves, freedom beyond reach, dahlia and peach reflected
in black sunglasses, all flowers and fruit
shimmer and dance in moments evaporated.
The taste returns to memory, and again
I reset the coil of my attention in attempt to touch
the center of my worrysome world and paint it fresh.

Our love is our *familiar* but we can't grab it by the scruff.
Our children walk alone on shaky ground, hearts on shirtsleeve.
We spend our lives hanging on only to surrender everything.
This irony has a taste just beyond reach but we teach them patience
and know this won't help when the time comes.
Get used to loss as a birthright and liberated outlook, what fun!

Peace in the middle-east is way beyond reach;
wiping out our enemies will fall short of achieving safety.
Our brother's hand can't grasp our own
while holding a rifle, black flag, open book, or clenched fist.

Election beyond reach of minorities fighting restrictive voter-laws.
What do we teach our children
if the nastiest and most bigoted wins by telling the same ol' big lies?
"Fool me twice" could be our campaign slogan, or "Too mean and unwise".

Crazy ways destroy our kids lives; continents out of reach in quarantine.
Low-brow rich men just beyond reach in penthouse suites
safe from the plague and poverty below.

A balanced checkbook is just beyond reach;
I can never figure out what went wrong, resort to balance adjustment.
Nothing quick about Quicken — Nothing ever reconciles.
Being debt-free a goal constantly moving one interest bump out of reach.
Banks with carrots hung out before pack-horse, sedative sugar cubes with a touch
of bitters. Back that new BMW into traffic to get in line and sit and wait.

Satisfaction beyond reach, beyond security, safety and pride.
Glorious minute imperfection adorns all proof and semi-permanence
kerfluffle meant to represent the ideal, just beyond reach.
Ground ever shaky, world spin dizzy-stoned with hurt, debt and cement.
Steel, glass, wood and wire puts real space beyond reach; real selves
compartmentalized into boxes that compose a sentence, an enforced calling.
Nature's *atman* rises above our own and holds us all
in a wisp of smoke, a hint of scent, all things fleeting and impermanent
fruit of the tree of life.
Seeds beyond reach, coiled spiral of universe strikes
at the leg of dark matter —
          Venom of dust and hot gas
    cures the absence
of arrival.
Cold womb of space
grows each definition
with a milk-ring of fire
around the aureole of
its mother's stellar breast
swollen for only so long.

That soft comfort beyond reach again as I drift off to sleep
a 50-something veteran of my generation's war with itself.
There is no treaty to be reached
we will just pass the torch on to the next letter
of the alphabet.

Generation G will be good for nothing.
Generation Q will question everything but get no answers.
Generation R will regret the path chosen by the Gs.
Generation T will toughen up for the singularity song
definitions beyond reach of imagination to conceive.

Prepare your kids, teach them to think
set them on a path of strong intent to achieve peace
with goals we can never see them reach
only smile from inside them as themselves
an inheritance of wisdom.
We are all Moses at our own mountaintops
and bid farewell to a promised land
we will never see.

The truth, so often just beyond reach
is a vague taste we can only season.
Tell your love what you've been withholding;
don't seize with reasons and be bold
if you want to touch heaven and to know
the value ring of that one thing within our reach:
for one moment to serve as all moments
and complete us, desireless.

Supplication to the Muse of the Dark Age

What must a mid-life crisis be like
for a 600 year old artist, a muse who has
lost all interest in her canvas;
hollow-cheeked muse, transfixed on the bottoms of her shoes
worn impossibly thin?

I find new respect for those who ride the edges
of themselves; who stretch to hear her voice
through the pipeline focus of a strained silence.
Pregnant stillness that shines too little light
into the growing din.

Momma's got a migraine and goes down for a century's nap
tries to avoid becoming alcoholic.
We can only lay flowers at the end of the bed and weep
for each child she suckled, sick with colic.
Partridge Mahjongg tiles jangle with loose change
while the angel baby chews on a rubber toucan
drops her plush moose in the tracks of cheese —
Creamed peas and yogurt in the kitchen lies uneaten.

Gloves are off in 2012, penultimate leg of the race
to the end of calendars — I cry out this supplication
as the eclipse begins and an eerie light is cast
to make her seem much further out of reach.

Please stay awake, keep your eye trained on us!
Be angry at the dull, drowsy pull of sleep for our sake;
for the sake of our brilliant children who thrash and
vomit and kick to fend off the loss of consciousness
jam their thumbs into their own eyes and scream
gullible innocence startled by their first hard winter.

Muse, teach me to be happy at sunset when light fades
and night's lonely sadness creeps across the floor;
a stupid serious tarp on twilight's mental woodpile
to always hew, split and stack more for the
coldest cold to come and then run out of Eden's echo
as a biting wind begins to blow.

We are alone and out of work on the grey gray street
under a gray grey sky, finally free of routine
but on the hunt for the next encumbrance.
Feed my ticket into the gleaming turnstile
put the next 50,000 miles on
year after year, each tax folder a different color.

Muse, only when your voice is heard can we see our enemies
else they stalk concealed and hungry for blood
sap our memory and surety, hapless bread unbuttered.
Books that are never read as they would never be understood
and never a word uttered that made any sense.
So Speak!

Do I have a secret? Weak security feeds the astral exploit.
Dark age replicates veils like a virus and we are
sick with infected eyes, pushing out of their sockets
from sour pollen, smog, sinus puff, soap opera sap and sob story.
A surreal, sullen fixation for the unemployed
a lost wheel without a map, revealed by the road
that speaks as an echo in passing —
          Can I remember to listen that hard?
          Will I ever be able to hear her clearly?

And what if I heard: *"A gas poison will descend like a biblical plague*
they'll blame Al Qaeda" — If you heard that
would you believe it?
Count the times the impossible has happened
sip bourbon mid-afternoon and play poker
evil cookies make laptop hot, drive spins
like Gentleman's Jack in my head.
I wait for the next niacin flush, the next club flush dealt.
Wind blows a blush into her cheeks peeking out
from the edge of the blanket
          — She is no longer impossible.

Repeat her name as a cryptic mantra
whispered at the ear as it ages and filters out the chaff
like a cat poised to pounce, ready to enslave it's prey.

O wild and beautiful one we are bound to protect, revive, enliven;
cultivate the spring trestle and employ all technology.
Vines curl in dreams you will not yet have

through nets self-cast, abundant teems of schools churn
in deep currents; you must pull each catch in close
before you know if it's a keeper. Sometimes
the bait bites *you* — O beautiful one, ocean reaper siren —
Garden multiplies from nothing into
a feast where water flows, cattle feed, veggies grow.

Slow walk down Zen path with morning coffee to sit
in quiet, damp pine while birds perk from sleep;
all to honor you as you please to hear my plea and
hold from reaping to let our fruit sweeten.
Let daddy get a job; fill the freezer with meat.

Signal fades
lost the call without getting the address of the interview
        — Damn.

Full force fall in a rain of leaves, crops trimmed
and drying in large bins; shrink wrapped sanity
convenient and hermetically sealed.
Last little green tomato at risk to ripen or rot before
winter frosts the cold stovepipe and eaves.
Try to talk sense so I hear you through the rain on the gutters
the sirens, derailments, hurricanes, flak —
        A mask surrendered is a
mask traded for another mask that masks the mask Jack.

I beg you to be revealed.

Hear my call so I don't lose you
in the muck and mire of this dark age.
Keep the rivers flowing in the veins of our close questions
to quench the rush and burn of aching blood.
Golden trees shed ruby leaves to swirl in a bright blue wind
that carries your name across the stage
in a rush of whispers.

Hear me when my breath gets thin
when the distance is long and the gap is wide
when cold is very cold and all is lost and grim.
Be the door and beacon above it to show the way
as the evening fog rolls in.

Demystifications

Plain Water

for Yuho

Six windows in the *zendo*
rain on them all, light growing through fog.
I tilt to one side and my leg comes alive again;
the tingling of blood like raindrops in my feet.

Plain water covering
and permeating all elements —
The news of the day is far less simple.

Plain water seduces me with its freedom.
Simplicity arrives like an ancient riverbed
yielding it's fossils without complaint.

Plain water interrupts the flow of thoughts
timed carefully on schedule —
The gong sounds — The world stops.

Plain water increases deliberate life
renewed on this day by our synergy
with a hidden midnight sun.

Plain water rolls around on an acrid tongue
pulled up and in, behind the teeth
motionless, mouthing a million inner voices.

Plain water, clear and perfect as a polished mirror —
Wooden clappers collide as *gassho* breaks the spell
reveals thundering silence.

What to Look At

The sadness of having loved and wanting love; of having money and wanting money of having tasted freedom and wanting freedom.

I'm looking at sadness at having tasted freedom and lost freedom;
of having tasted love
and lost love; of having had money and lost money.
I'm looking at women's sacrifice for love of me; all sentient beings as my mother.
I'm looking at women who loved me and lost me; women who love me
and will lose me; money that will be lost; deeper engagement
that limits freedom.
I'm looking at the enmeshment of these things, roving eye-trap hypnotized —
    Scent of various women down a street that reeks of love, money
    entrapment and loss.
I'm looking at a lovely young woman I'd love to love and know I'll lose her.
I'm looking at the fold of money from my pocket; numbers on statements, balances
    already bid adieu.
I'm looking at the crawl of my progress toward freedom and I know the race is lost.
I'm looking through window glass to a sprawling mountain field.
I'm looking at my home of contradiction.
I'm looking through a perfect glass, onto a perfect field and feel perfect;
    perfectly at a loss to say what it is I am really looking at, what it is I see that
    would make me want to get dressed and go outside to walk.
I'm looking at the loss of city to mountain field.
I'm looking at the loss of country to concrete spires.
I'm looking at a field and think I have something to say.
I'm looking at a field and know I have nothing to say — I am at a loss.
I have lost fields — I have lost cities.
I'm looking at creation catching me here wherever that is.
I'm looking at all the women who've loved me and then lost themselves in loving me.
I'm looking at their eyes all looking at me
as I look out through the window glass at a field of towering sunflowers
    under which I maze.

*

I'm not looking at her square pout, on the verge of hysterical tears, right before torrents come; that very moment of loss, bad news that changes everything. Wonder lost, heaven sound drowned, song gone minor; all woes invoked by day and kept in a satin pouch with a mirror and her favorite ticket stubs.

I'm looking at the big picture behind an attractive veil.
Butter melts on a porcelain plate;
plate warms on a pewter tray; tray scuffs an oak table and so on
deeper and deeper down to the
Sumerian creation myth where Nibiru slew Tiamat and the asteroid belt
was formed and the comets were sent on their giant orbits.

I'm not looking everywhere for that one good thing, golden fleece, perfect partner;
reasonable fatherly tutelage defining my education for the "real" world.
I'm not looking at a world of pain; I'm opening a tin can of air and letting cats
out of bags, rabbits from hats, birds from deep black sleeves —
Mercury rising and falling in sun's wake.

I'm not looking at a watch to tell time; can't rely on stiff hands to define
a productive schedule — There's a bonny brook running through a Gaelic wood
and I have nothing at all to do with it.
I sacrifice time to an altar of breaths;
each breath a finite duration, every piece of the whole a fractionary hologram.

I'm not looking at an eternal reward to redeem my failure;
a big couch or soft knee of god to bounce my soul on when breath gives out.
Carapace rocket behemoth arcing through space
cannot clear the table of these dirty dishes, wash out stains made by errors of omission.
Sound of footsteps coming down the hall with a tremendous verdict —

What to look at:
Loss, abandonment, geography, pain, clocks
rope tricks, streams through dense woods;
rocket stage of divine illusion disengaged —

Waves slowly whisper up the beach
wake-ripple fades into moon lake
as reflection clarifies.

Real Shenpa Granma

"There are Rubins in the raindrops;" she said
"someone puts on the lights and goes out of the house and leaves me alone."
Wants wrinkle cream for 100 yr old face;
shows broad phony smile to strangers
but not a one for her daughter
whom she did not like
and it was mutual.

Self-absorbed with her looks and with money
she never found anything funny about spending
even for Ensure to keep her from wasting away;
she'll be the wealthiest skeleton at her own funeral as they say.

Ironic that mom was the one who took care of her at the end —
A final trip for pastrami and knishes at the Mill Basin Deli in Brooklyn
and to see her sister Phyllis whom she
also could not stand
and now her legs themselves
won't allow the same.

Two absent sons coddled as darlings but as uncaring
as self-absorbed, as concerned with #1
or with who gets the couch when she goes.
Only attachment to the familiar remains;
the price difference on a can of peaches
between Waldbaums and Key Foods.

Throwing hospice out onto the street
she cannot read intent or fine print or faces.
Maintains kosher and eats no meat
to ease the silver-red ravage of psoriasis
yet absent-mindedly ate salami and cheese at the holidays right off the tray —
No one dare tell her.

Left leg leaking through the compression sock
onto the floor in a puddle she wipes all day long
with a rubber clog on washrag —
Half her weight since last year
yet heart strong as a bull eating only salad and
Entenmanns Chocolate Chip Pound Cake.

Holding fast to her last shreds of identity;
won't take her meds, throws them around the kitchen "for what!?"
"1-2-3-4-5-6-7-8-9 pills — I won't take em!"
Who can argue with an old woman who has lived through seven wars
the depression, a century of disappointment —
Her dusty violin in the corner
memories in the bow threads, the sheep gut strings;
the unavoidable passing of all things.

Before she died in Bellevue after two weeks, no food or water
a foot in both worlds, of two minds, shallow breath starts and stops;
she spoke aloud to her dead aunt Esther, then told me in dreamtime
        "I'm saying my farewells ... if you need me you can find me in-between
the raindrops...

I will be more fearless next time."

Damn Impatience

I can't make it all happen right now and
I'm damn sick and tired of it!

Gotta wait 3:25 for popcorn to pop in microwave.
Had to wait forty-two years for my soulmate to show up
on Match.com — Nearly missed her
        in digital apathy of a decaying online profile
        with a three month halflife.

Gotta wait for the train again — That damn 6:46 is
always 10 minutes late.
Gotta wait to get paid; "check's in the mail…"
Gotta wait years for a paltry 3% bond yield.

Gotta wait my turn at the post office
while Matilda is paying for a book of stamps
        with small change.
Have to wait forty years to return to Naropa for my MFA?!
Had to raise three kids, start and fold three businesses.
Lawrence Ferlinghetti, I'm still waiting for a rebirth of wonder!

Can't wait for the muse to drop her sparkling guano in my lazy eye!
Can't wait for Friday end of business; thumb-start the Harley and ride.
Can't wait for next Monday's first date;
can't wait for her to call — Come sit on my face, get to know me!

I can't wait for the lightning bolt of love to strike my heart this very instant!

I need it all at once; *all* gourmet delicacies; *all* herbal euphorias.
I need her all at once; her whole body in my mouth from nape to sacrum.
I can't stand not having enough; can't stand not getting what I want!
Can't stand to wait on lines; I'd never make it in a communist land.
I want it all right now, I want my bird in the hand!

Gotta wait for the market to improve before I sell Telecoms.
Gotta wait for next year to get a raise when advertising improves.
Gotta wait for my ship to come in;
        foghorn blast through thick Hudson mist echoes —

I can't wait for my impatience to resolve
into radiant presence that has nothing pending.

I can't wait for the money to publish more poetry.
        There's never enough money for poetry!

Gotta wait for digestion to finish so I can be hungry again.
Gotta wait for the maze hedge to grow opaque so we can get lost and be found.
Gotta wait for trans-humanist cyborg implants that will make me all powerful.
Gotta wait for science to decode my gangly genome.
Gotta wait for the great cure that ends all plagues.
Gotta wait for the *Elohim* to land again
        Annunaki of the radiant *Shem* — Winged disk to rise
when all waiting will be over and
        'neither shall there be any more death'.

God's Funeral

The most that can be expected
when ideas die
is a loving cup of
bitter irony at their end;
the modest means to have a
spare suit dry cleaned
and sit thoughtfully
before a corpse.

What can we do
however
when the most sacred roots
are torn from
ground eroded by twenty bloody centuries flow
exposing how shallow they grow?

We are recently invited to
witness the death of god;
the unmasking of the monist
with demystified certainty
that there is no one single bearer of thunderbolts;
no absolute feisty old codger with a baseball bat
broom, or cigar;
no one to save us from ourselves
from the singularity, point of no return.

Sobbing in the front row is
the rabbi from my bar mitzvah
who thought he was a Mossad agent
in a pedophilic prance across the dance floor;
a white suited fatcat tv preacher who stuck his brimstone
where he oughtn't without a second thought and
with many second comings; many second helpings
at the feast before lent
with a host of pious thirty-something virgins
who bitterly repent.
I glided over to the canapés and munched the duck confit.
Happy to be free of the source of all guilt, I added another pat of butter
to my Irish soda bread and was even happier for it.
That small reduction in stress has extended my life.

Ever since god had gotten sick, the exposed hypocrisy
had made us all uneasy.
It's better this way, he's finally at peace, the world has
spun completely out of control and that's
just the way it needs to be right now.

Surely someone's ripe to take the reins; guide us over
this hump of repeating history
before it's too late.
Once again we course into a
weak kink in the vein of body politic.
God's stroke knocked us all off our feet;
we thought he'd bounce back but no dice.
We imagined no possessions, buried nuclear battleaxe
in caves of Afghanistan.
We hoped the maker would see us through but instead
here we are kissing his holy ass goodbye.

Let us please have a moment of silence for god
and wish him innocent good luck on the infinite cosmic ribbon.
Let us coop ourselves up in the mountain house and tell his heroic stories
contemplate his impermanence and lift a glass.
Let's hear it for god, once and future king, gone 4 now, so sorry, see ya later —
Here's hoping you can live through this, cope with everything;
get through the burial, survive as long as you can.

Buck up kiddo it's not so bad; you've inherited the vacuum.

The Day Before I Die

The day before I die will be a day like any other;
the deep reciprocity
of cognition
absolute abandonment of security.
No recourse, no escape, no purpose other than
eventualities, small complaints, small senses.

It will be a morning like any other.
I will make some bacon.
I will remember an old Beatles song.
I will choke up easily.
I will drop the soap and stoop in the shower
to pick it up and put it back on the rack.

Blank canvas alert is just a firework of the mind.
I cannot restrain myself any longer.
Suffering has kindled my rage and awareness is
just a bitter pill that cannot cure or even be swallowed.

If it weren't a day like any other
I would worry I was being paranoid as usual and this
persistent pain in my heart was a mere phantom murmur.

I will ignore my "precious human birth" urgency as usual
and do my best to be comfortable and warm.

I will sit and think of all the things I need to do
and plan how to make something happen, anything at all.

I will look out the deck windows and scan the fallen trees
again and trace the path of squirrels and snowy woodpeckers again.

I will wonder if the plants need water.
I will give dat fat cat more nuggetz.

I will eat a piece of prosciutto or honey ham or mortadella
or Wunderbar Bologna right out of the open meat drawer.

I will build a fire in the wood stove and light a stick of pine incense.
I will check my email too many times.

I will pack a bowl and dream that familiar high.
I will walk out on the deck and look up at the sky; Orion's belt and North Star.

I will pour myself a shot of Jack and put my feet up;
watch a cooking show or two.

It will be a day like any other though
an uneasy sense of distant storms brewing.

I have been running out of time since the day I was born.
I have made my bed and will sleep in it finally

but first I will stretch, roll joints, windmill and crack my bones as I've done every night since I was a theatre student.

In the end I might die of incredulity.
I just can't believe this place and the way lives go.

In the end there's just no way to know;
you just keep going toward the penultimate moment

something ordinary, something almost final.
You can laugh or cry it doesn't matter a bit to Father Time.

I will find my refuge finally in poetry and in family
as there are few things that truly take my breath away.

See you tomorrow; I'll let you know, or not.
We can sit and have a bowl of Guava Skunk and chat

and under a violet twilight sky, eat a meat sandwich or a sundae
and somehow say a proper, unspoken goodbye.

Ponderance

For so long
I have been no one.
Elusive mind anchors itself
like an obstinate child
that cannot be budged.

Pure lust and tantrums;
No forest — No trees.

Someday I will die
and Nothing will become
clear.
Only on
the edge
do we
realize
Nothing.

Maybe I will echo
like the instant after
a bell peals;
a death
resonate in limitless aftermath
of absence.

Every illness brings us closer to the end
of a very long
outbreath —

What takes its course takes
everything
and what remains takes
the rest.

Zazen

Say nothing about desire;
be silent about your needs.
'Mum's the word' on possible partnerships;
button your lip about the *Elohim*.
Zip it up about the mighty second coming;
not a word about the silver bird.
Quiet about what you've always really wanted;
put a lid on everything your father said.
Clamp down on the most beautiful disappointment;
kill sleep, deny rest, refuse refuge.
Buddha falls by the side of the road;
lilies and tulips close in moonless night
bowed with no memory of sun
no anticipation of being lifted again
and then . . .
          in the flash of an eye
                    I am an old man
          reminiscing about old loves
                    wins, losses and could'a beens
books filled with resistance
and memory of resistance.

Little did I know that, graduating alone
we take a seat in an invisible college.
On and on, lesson after lesson it goes
to peel the wrappers off an innate knowledge
that cannot be learned.

A rat scurries down a train rail
by icy Hudson in hollow echo
of a riveredge factory hum — Tankership
at dock unloading fuel; classic 1940s
limousine with huge whitewalls groans by
on country gravel.
Doves, wrens and cardinals peck
at a cage of seed and suet cake
that hangs on a still bare spring branch
swayed in early breeze.

Zen is strong — Zen is weak.
No muscle can lift
the unsurpassable.

Stone Wall Bench

Carved totem among weeds
groaning air conditioners sweat on a gravel laid path.

Clean windows reflecting
hidden sprinkler spigot rainbow mist.

Mosaic bark of huge maple
dendritic herbs drying in hot mile-high sun.

Naropa brecciated megalith
holding Colorado fossil.

The way her hips sway
up the wooden ramp to the Day House.

Rubber teeth of mountain bike
biting and chewing asphalt.

On the Green River at Brattleboro
Maple steam rising over muddy covered bridge echoing basketballs

or Sugarloaf Mountain at daybreak
reservoirs like mirrored eyes looking up.

My cat Torus has a field day
carefully stepping through sand along a precipice of mint.

Boulder Renga

Electric socket
orange & white
makes shadows

feelings flowing
through the mind like clouds.

Sharp risk of sun
breaks & enters the room
without shame

blue shirt
glows gold.

A new type of socket
directed upwards
to unlimited energy.

The Reiki of electricity
burns down the line.

Tree shine
sap is buzzing
chlorophyll electrons.

The sacred mountain.
The goddess of the spirulina.

Juice in blender
green after rain
Max the cat crunches kibble.

Icy bananas
roaring on blades.

Between oasis, monkeys & mountains
I hesitate for a moment
& then walk on.

Crunch of trail
dips into silent canyon.

Cotton clouds
silver soar
over green ground

and thunder
destroys the temple.

We mourn the sacred
flags fray
in the whip of aftermath.

Flagpoles turn to spires
comb the sky.

With Darrell Jonsson & Pavla Jonssonova

Demystifications

The entire meaning of life is to pay the purchase price
for everything; cover the total nut —
Buy the farm and till the farm and feed the till;
hew a family from dust.

Tossed before life like dice down
        a long alleyway;
the proposition that we can recover
        from any loss
invites chance —
                Your hands shake as you hold her picture frame.
                She's hysterical on the phone over nothing.
                She can't stop making insulting phone calls.

I can barely stand the human drama let alone
an angel's summoning embrace.

Who, if I cried, would hear me anyway?

Bulging magazine rack sweats fiction.
Small mirrors in the sunglass turnstile reflect arcade strobes.
She turns around the corner in the fun house and is gone.
Small mirrors demystify the echo of her blue-shadowed eye.

What could she ever do, take me back?
I always thought leaving meant 'everything shed'
completely empty; going out of business hollow
        "to the last sale!"

Coping with denial — One great big desire
sum of so many little desires; secret message
at the bottom of your coffee cup, bullseye
at the bottom of your saké cup.

Opening mail at breakfast
an unemployed Minneapolis love poet writes:
        "Nobody loves me."
Her poems were bleary-eyed and tender; made me cry.

Denny's waitress on Baseline in Boulder
said unprompted as she
topped off my mug:

"The heart is the storm;
the brother you lean upon, the rock
face of the holy spirit.
Seasons and the weather are always
changing into the rainbow.
The groin is the quake, your father;
land where you land at point zero.
This is all there is to life.
Love is our eyes through five senses.
If I can't wonder through your tears
then I see only animals."

"There is something," she says
                                        her violet eyes sparkling with an infant purity
"somewhere roads meet within your soul
and energy accumulates there."

Music filled the cutter's dark cave; stone to self-same lap sings.
        Cleave crystal to uncover the order most high
        soften my mysteries with science.
Get me safe into the cutter's magnified eye with a generous loupe
to examine and demystify
her ardent visage.
Eye gems
facet lashes brilliant
from inside.
Cold sun
on strata of pavement
        demarks
a path to my name.

Forged seal upon the frame of
tree entrance, ripening fruit overhang —

        "You must change your life;" he said
        encircling the torso of Apollo
        "you must stand
                before the great and glorious

figure of self in stone
                    mirroring and becoming".
Cassiopeia was
another star he named
          like women tightly strung
in suspension spans of his love;
held up under massive skies
          re-lit as fusions of sorrow
          to other, safer shores —
  Yet among these winters you are most endlessly winter.

There are people we
invite to wound us
opening our hearts to them
like sluices to their rivers;
filtered gems and heavy stones
our delightful burden
our dark center.

The Nature of Impermanence Haunts Me

The nature of impermanence haunts me as the first fall leaves crisp and pass before my window on their way down.

It's 2:36PM and all is lost and
just begun;
a nice big Berkshire pork shoulder
smoking on my Napoleon.

I am watching a hippo
eat a pumpkin on Facebook;
the broken branch remains
in evening sun illuminated.

Before I know it
I will be in the ground
or ash in a crucible;
smelted soul risen.

An orb spinner strung from spruce to trellis
spends hours building his intelligent design.
Ida spins and avocados fall;
the orb becomes a hurricane flag.

The wind takes everything
and by nature it makes you sad;
pollenating the world with flowers
and dust of crumbled monuments.

We are already gone
but remain as a smell, a scattered shadow
some dust in a ray of light;
a taste of smoke on the tongue
unctuous fat, sticky skin.

My low knee buckles on the stairs, coffee spills.
Small piece of sun on grass.
October sets in hard.

*

Deep karmic attachments, an inner grotto;
roots of passion, aggression and ignorance echo.
Fear is ignorance and ignorance, fear.
Solvent of illness breaks the spell.

Through the eye of a thousand needles
we ripple into a myriad of selves far from home
only to fall and land again and again
unable to sew our story together end to end.

Slip through the keyhole of twilight;
narrowly escape Covid again.
Sight is steam, a beginning wreck
of statues, societies, the silken clock.

Germantown Oneness Center Zen Retreat

what the light brings
what the rain brings
what silence brings
what incense brings
what a train whistle brings
what red grapes after zazen brings
what a spider plant brings
            swaying in front of white curtains
what a red sun brings
what a ticking clock brings
what a beeper brings
what white pine brings
what the flat spine brings
what a mirror brings

Zazen Weekend at the Grail

Sitting as Buddha
behind the shrine
between angled windows;
watching mind and
dual incense streams
rise & curl
like rams horns
in Aries gray spring.
Deer ticks leap from tree bark
to truck their miniature dose of Lyme
into the truck stop of loose socks hanging
over a row of hiking boots.

Hold cosmic mudra below my navel
for another quiet hour until the gong
and then *kin hin* walking like mountains
over slick, creaking floorboards.

Crack blank book of Zen
leaf through endless memories.
Fertile ground pounds behind
eyes on the spot
to photosynthesize attachment
into boundless simple awareness.

Every loss a gain
silence invites inner ear thunder.
Expanded mind, a sponge saturated
responds to a good squeeze.

I take back whatever suffering I may have caused
and offer my folly unto emptiness.
I take it all back.

I take back parquet floor varnish reflection
as you walked across it toward me with your eyes closed.
I didn't stop you in time and you ran right into me.
I could've stopped you but I didn't.
I take back the failed trust exercise.

I take back my childhood oppressors — Zeb Apostolakis, Doug Levy, Adam Stark
when I stand up for my daughter being teased on the school bus.
Punk whispers "Bitch" and "Crack Baby", pencil point hitting her in the cheek
makes my blood boil.

I take back the lonely shuffleboard afternoon in Miami
from an elderly future in some alternate determinate.
Hock up phlegm in new millennium first quarter century
arrive too quickly to the next promised land.

I take back my trickle charger, my gem kiln, my lapidary bench
these tight shoes; wrong size Levis, all safeties, catalogs, windchimes.
I take back the sweet image of your face as we lay in bed, you
slack jawed and vibrating, wrinkled smiling grimace up in smoke.
I take back the photograph of you by the alder tree looking sideways like an angel.
I take back every good idea I ever had that you tried to take credit for.
I take back the job that castigated me into salesman's hell with nowhere to go
nothing to sell.
I take back what I lost in disillusioned post-teen anxiety on the rillorah of
a beautiful melonball chomper debutante taffeta lap dance in a private booth.
I take it all back.

A flock of wild turkeys crunch
methodically through
falling leaves
        in the woods behind the Grail
        on their way to an open field.

We sit with Yuho's koan: *"Am I led by doubt or by faith?"*
I am no closer to an answer
yet closer to myself for asking.

Crows hit their square note squarely
and swoop —
        Carob and dried oak displace
as the path tightens into a maze.
Breeze blows communal kitchen curtains;
a recipe for poise, squash porridge
with currants & cranberry steams.
Warm November geese
huddle in flight.

Pieces of Tears

Little wedges of sadness
keep open the door to my heart.
I am endlessly feeling.

Familiar faces of friends
who once faced me
are figured all over my
instruments of memory
like music.

There is a clear light of
goodness somewhere
present
in my being
                    yet
so help me
sometimes
I wonder.

A piece of my tears falls
upon my hand
          and there is a piece
                    that never lands.

Naropa Tent Walk

Frayed sandal scrapes
black tipped match, piece of pine twig.
Dot-matrix accordion fold tear-offs the only
cheerleader pompom here —
Raindrops smack into my leg
by the rainbow banner, raindrops
on the page smear ink from wet wooden pen.
Storm winds slam tent flaps against poles;
mountain bike poised to ride straight up
the side of the building — Stomach talks;
    door to the music room is padlocked and
    man in a dress smokes where dogs
    are not allowed.

White cotton pollen falls on green leaves
as sun returns —
I lie down among bees;
black and yellow monarchs
flit over bustling anthills and poppies
arch their slender necks without a hint of sleep.
Tiny eyes tremble into a cool home of sand —
    Weathered wood stairs hold
    corners of dried leaves and straw;
old webs, bark and paint chips
against red brick —

Clouds moving low over Flatirons
part to let sun hit its crest of pine.
Bike tires on sand crackle
every road; blue umbrella beads rain
and rolls off —

Red roof glistens — Hidden moon is lit;
iron grate patios packed with gravel and
crushed leaves rust —
Rain begins again, this wooden pen
sets roots into my hand and grows.
    Weeds sprout in abandoned flowerpots;
    sun breaks through
    to complete their feast —

Sandals crack twigs;
garden stakes lie flat pointing to the gate.
Compost simmers as a host to Universe
and ochre wildflowers like a robe over
shoulders of a thousand wheels that carry the road.

Schema

A multileveled revelation
of who, what, why, when, where, and how
this whole damn reality was conceived
and what its actual purpose is amid the
schematic of so many grand schemas;
the dreams we never realize and must release
that nevertheless live on.

The brightness of this pain is wondrous.
The fan spins and inside lights change temperature
relative to the sun.
Titles on book spines glow
and mean nothing and everything at once.
Actual dream is a rock that never changes
only spins like everything does.

We are dream rock, book spine, bright pain, spinning fan.
We live on without any answers
and there you go, there's your schema;
live dizzy in that painful spinning question if you can.

The heart of the universe breaks
for itself constantly;
we all know what's happening
without speaking of it.
Shadows fall across our eyes with age;
old habits never fade
but stand from early on
if our parents are silent.

Once the parent is gone
clouds blow through and take their
shape at moments
a watchful yet impotent eye.

The broken heart of the universe
never mends by design.
Lessons unlearned lined up in the queue
pull you forward into
the round mirror of an ancient and familiar face

silent, bright, broken and watching you.
Dream ache echo dissolves into bittersweet sigh.
Grass, weeds, and flowers all grow wild.

Another Guise

Stocks

I buy Apple, Adobe, Cisco, Oracle, Immune Response; another guise
of the highly refined long strategy, watch
five HDTV screens and the ticker simultaneously.
Japanese entertainment industry bondsmen
cluster around high screens on dark kiosks.
Columbian emerald mines, Chinese sea cucumbers, biotech chip implants —
Cell Genesys, Waste Management, HBO—MTV, Capital Cities oil glut —
Fiber-optic telecom, Holographic teleportation, T-cell receptor geometry —
Superconductive materials transcend the earth wave.
Call Ed Clark, buy Montana jade mines and sapphire bars.

I've already got plans for the profits from the
first million carats:
10000 to Naropa — 10000 to Karma Triyana Dharmachakra —
10000 to Crestone retreat — Coffee shop in Las Vegas —
Maybe a diner within pacific wave reach, carrier pigeon legion
all carrying *Om Mani Padme Hum* scrolls.

Golden sangha
like a triple–gem Hollywood band of influence
like the bondsmen
adhering in concentric rings emanating from the
        one holy guru.
All else is charnel ground, a feast for crows.

Rejected salesmen wander through
halls of chrome elevators and moving stairs
seeking pure goddesses of porcelain in the polished glass;
Romeo–Prometheus species moving in dark fabrics
through endless aisles and rows of wanting to get to know you
to know your business and to make it their mask.

Take stock of the precious commodity of balance
here among skyscrapers and iron doors.
Thousands after thousands of doors opening and closing
like game pieces accumulating into millions of tons of cities
our shares of the market in rock.

Skinheads march in Oregon, Idaho, Virginia.
Separatists stock weapons of erasure

dead–brain arrogance, criminal hatred
as an investment in heartbreak.
Sad, self–made victims cower and tremble
as vampirous mini–despots devour their world
like a virus, pollute the righteous, pure nature
they claim to defend; a total, non–discriminating nature
exuding the antibody, antidote of seasons, time passing
in renewal as they march to the tune of anti–prayer
hands held high to burning midnight.

Will the fool, this goddess's child
remember his weapon and tear through
the aorta of this iron body, slice the hangman's noose
rethrow the only vase for his one white rose?

Will the market remember to crash when
all hands are stirring the poison soup, when
Earth's management takes a poison pill to
avoid the takeover of all things truly valuable?

Americade Suite

Mustang ferry
the Minne-Ha-Ha blasting three horns
as she backs out
onto Lake George.

Song about an "Old Man"
touches me and fingers push
through matted gray
like slips lined up along the coast.

Song about being a "Friend of the Devil"
says the woman catches up with you
and you end up in jail.
Well, not if I can help it;
they got her on Felony Criminal Mischief
scratched my car up with her key.
I'll trade everything for a 32 foot motorhome
and hit the road; she'll never find me.

Vermont 'graduation' teddy bear gift bungied
to sissy bar riding down Rt. 7
from Burlington. F-5 Ferry over
Lake Champlain, thinking about
the women in my life —
        Got 4 bars of cellphone reception.
        Called my broker at Fort Ticonderoga;
        sold out of MUSE at a profit
        sold puts on Oracle — She put me down.
        Pessimism is winning now.

Depressed and rolling in it.
Snap of a fringe flap and brake tick;
bear button air hole, small acrylic tuft of paw
peeks out — My burrito wants very much to pour
out of me overboard.

I kick back on the porch of the
Inn on The Hill smoking a nice
2-hour Robusto like
Don Sebastien; a keg can of Heineken
close at hand.

Watch moonrise over the lake.
Dozens upon dozens of bikes
of all types parade by —
Leather, rubber, black silk and
red lipstick my downfall.
I keep a shiny side up
and dry socks in my boots.
Mars rises and the unread emails pile up;
she's not pregnant after all
or won't be for long.

Rt. 74 past Paradox
through Severence
and into Speculation.
S curves wake me from
my dream of gravity.
Fireworks last 1/2 Hr.
on Prospect Mt., inspire
patriot's elegiac compromise
'Those who died to make us free.'

None of Us Are Free

None of us are free
nor would we if we could be.
Baby's eyes roll up and back;
sweet jaw pump on nipple
shows a glimpse of that joyous bliss
that eclipses us from birth to death.

My girl is magic
the benefit of my enmeshment
and with one hand on her sated cheek
I write this
swelled with more than I
can comprehend.

Time stands still single-handed.
Futon dries on the overcast deck.
She sleeps in my lap
cries out from a fitful dream
and dives in again.

If this is not freedom
then all waters are dark and to hell
with tomato blight; menacing orb spinners
set their giant nets across the stair rail.
Avocado tree cranes to capture the last days
of summer's light
and I know only
that life refuses to fail
to be constrained
to meet expectations;
drained of every last ounce of energy
you ever thought you would be required to muster.

Morning sleep broken by her sweet face and suddenly
an overflow of feces everywhere —
In a flurry of wipes
metallic citrus rot rises to hit the fan;
cat howls for a can.
Labor Day's list of endless labors
down for a nap.

Mommy Mafia

The ones with nicer clothes set the tone.
When they hate Cuomo and love Trump
you'd better too or face the angry mob
be the ghost mom, cold shoulder faucet drip-drip.

Idiot chromosome
for cavewoman dominance;
toxic coffee clatch code of silence
vilifies the odd mom out.

Hold your tongue in mixed company;
you never know who is listening and
may judge you or keep your daughter
from the next birthday party.

This catty omertà side-glance bitch wall
builds brick by delusional brick —
I load my slingshot with a space laser
and keep my distance so as not to get sick.

Anti-vax, anti-lib, anti-gay, anti-antifa;
pro-life, pro-Trump, pro-white, pro-wall.
They got mean kids, just like them, sponges of toxic bias.
Anyone you don't see at church on Sunday is made of glass.

Sorry-ass obese prance at poolside
to cheer the fastest swimmer by chanting snide comments
at the slowpoke, mommy outside to catch a smoke;
spit drips down her locker door.

So odd a town filled with cops and firefighters
would be the epitome of intolerance.
Wait…that's not so odd after all;
after all, the white family sits down to have a bite

and reinforce the fantasy of an American dream
without any Jews, Hispanics or people of color.
We are rubbed out, fit with cement boots; we gotta go, it's curtains.
We swim with the fishes, retrieve our pot luck dishes.

Black Smoke Rising

Belladonna crackwhore purple needle vein papacy.
Rock-and-roll undergarment hocus-pocus papacy.
Back against the wall, below the belt papacy.
Beat to the punch line, the bread line, the conga line papacy.
Silver tray, muddy-handed, own-your-soul papacy
that barks, bites and cleaves arrested miters
works the crowds like Merlin to seduce an opportune waif
with table laden heavy, gilded and rare marbled papacy.

Where to now, Saint Peter?
Empty echoes from the hollow apse
headless hagiarchy moaning for its own
arms reaching into robes, pockets, dockets, waving blind at walls
horsemen waiting for the nod of Apocalypse, hooves stamping.
No pills or frills stop-drop-and-roll-out-more lunacy.
More brown worker bees, drones in the belt of the bible lunacy.
Babies are parish breadbasket collection dimes, can't you see?
Women cut cloth (but can't wear cloth) hetero-lunacy
"produce or die" damnation for men married in fruitless hell.

Black smoke
no pope — radio — HA!
We now know
what he really did in the woods —
The haze clears
reveals a neo-badass storm trooper theologian on the balcony.
The people's fears are tied to sacrifice under papal hegemony.
Apostles remind bumpkins to presidents just what
and where and who and why the rapture and salvation — yadda yadda
but never how to survive a flood
never cross their own desert or climb their Everest
never eat of the fruit of the tree of knowledge
only point to the moon as they say,
blinded by the finger, "*moon is invisible.*"

Veiled by the pat on the head 'there-there' papacy.
Burnt at the stake — *nothing really at stake* papacy.
Magna Carta salivating at the colonial bit papacy.
Virtue in viceless silence papacy.
ETWN airbrushed knuckles pressed in 24hr powdered reverie
sweating guests ever-dressed for God's prom.

A degree in catholicity, a book of blacked-out pages.
Read only what fits on the head of a pin
the diplomacy of bread for belief.
Give us your dancing feet, your braceleted necks, your cross-hitched hands
and we will give you proper hooves
bowed shorn heads
itchy whites
Clorox to memory
your whittled corpse on a stick, to replace
bonfires of joy.
Kill to convince;
conversion is kind.
Promise not to touch self or other
and leave all of you for me papacy.

Verses crammed into heads like leaves into lawn bags
blackbirds in the pie bursting to fly out
(papacy remains silent).
Chanted and beaten and whacked and lectured papacy
changes its tune, backs out, into a corner, up against the wall.
A pinned-down papacy
braying lack of interest, feigned poverty, frayed golden thread in
the hem of the gown.
Dance for the king and queen, the president, butcher, baker, and thief—
Earth a spinning ball of mirrors and
a hundred million sacrifices a minute,
spirits colliding against the gates of Eden.

A hair's breadth from decadence, the patient, pregnant pause
that holy halo of friar fringe smoke plume
negative space of nuclear mushrooms huge.
That comet crater seconds before centrifuge
the funhouse of pompacy, emperor's robes, bare-assed for those who see
mirrors suggesting gold-toothed smiles, toned calves
those gassed chants of mother-may-I, ignored
the coming-in-seconds, the incoming blow.

Rapturous virgin diversion of vanishing feats
is taken, rescued, redeemed, released
but the pope stays in his basilica without consensus—
Her first menses stain the burlap pillow she clenched
as god himself entered her over and over—

Abase the shrine no more, air out the manger, and for god's sake
open a window on this world you made
if you can bear the stench.
Decry the prattle, preach, ply, buck by buck papacy.
Needle sinks into the vein and it's all better papacy.
Battle cry to beat the converted with their own shameful limbs
until they too cry, *"We forgive!"* — *"We Surrender!"*

"defender of the faith of life please wake us from this terrible dream!"

Howling wind carries a thin myrrh across Europe, America and seven seas.

With Jacqueline Ahl

236

236 E. 36th St. my father's NY address
for 23 years
                now 15 years gone
and still coming through
with echo of
numerological synchronicity
shows me
we never die
just recalculate.

"Inspected by 236 "
shows up in a
pair of new jeans
2:36 the exact time on the clockradio
as I stare at gaining sun on cold muddy wheatfield
out a pollendust-clouded springtime window
during a sweet Hendrix solo.

236 countries in the world and all of them have money.
Bloomberg reports: Boston has over 235,000 high tech workers;
1000 errant techies making their way through the Berkshires.

236 bones in the body of my old cat.
236, my phone extension at work.
$237.36 in my checking account
today after paying child support.

I put in Joni Mitchell's "Turbulent Indigo" —
The first cut " Sunny Sunday" is 2:36 min. long.

April 2000 issue of Hot Bike magazine
"Biggest Issue Ever!"
"236 Pages of Harley-Mania!"

Optima charge from G & G Leather
for drum-dyed, naked cow black leather
highway jacket: $235.93 —
        Seven cents from cool —

U.S. President George Bush and his four top advisers
made a combined total of 237 misleading public statements
on the threat posed by Iraq.

Republicans pushed a $2.36 trillion budget through the Senate this year;
a package allowing lower spending and smaller tax cuts than President Bush
wants and trimming record deficits faster than he proposed.

Invoice amount billed to Synergy Healthcare
for my layout and mechanical of
Wall Street Journal European Edition ad
promoting a Prague banking institution: $236.25.

Digital broadcast television uses a black digital count of 16 and a white
digital count of 235 in order to provide a larger encoded color gamut.
One white pixel tarnished on the threshold of approximation.

In the van to the train depot
big red semi
cruising down 17 Quickway;
decal of white numbers knocked out
on hood of front cab: "236".

My NY Thruway EZ-Pass account number: 2361901.
Final Brady's Repair bill for old Honda Accord: $236.37.

Sitting here at 12:36 pm in front of my Quadra 950 —
236,044 bytes transferred just now in my Super Kermit download
from Minnesota BBS of the new U-MAX PlugInScan Utility v. 3.6.

Invoice number on Times Herald Record
bill for my classified ad placed
to sell old lapidary equipment: 236983-361190.

8 oz. of Blue Chamomile massage oil = 236 ml
for my feet and elbows.

Walking down 5th ave. toward the Nuyorican Poet's Cafe (236 E. 3rd St.)
feeling introverta-blue
and wondering what to do
with myself;
I ducked into Burke & Burke
for a couple of raspberry *rugelach* —

Baggy on the scale:
Net Wt. .20 lb.
Unit Price: $11.80 per lb.
Price lights up: $2.36 —
I choked on my Ben & Jerry's Apple Pie Frozen Yogurt
engaged in a harmony of numbers that verifies
how hard I work.

Nature always more than we know, always a surprise.
Conceived self only mirrors cloudy reflections
through flashes of auspicious coincidence —
We never die
just recalculate

and Lou Hirsch;
not my father anymore but my
advance man in the Bardo of Becoming
come through again with ghostly abacus.

Aspects Wither

Aspects wither as a winter fire shrinks and sputters.
The pilot light small, blue, and on standby with
everything else pending; a baby in my wife's belly.
Still unknown heart floats in its womb-bubble
removes the cell restriction, its sheath of limited purity
and flows down the channel of suffering
to its own ironic dawn; unique cry builds a
latent weapon that must be fed to be armed.

The assortment settles like tendencies in a nut case
stands with no resolution; no rest to the cycle of winds
that tear through these leaves, sprung with holes eaten
by new autumn aphids and mites birthed by the mother plant
that pushes its young up through the decomposition
to jump from the rotting to the reborn; green shoots sun eye
cranes to catch the day's dollop of warm salvation.
A cough fades in fluid, the feet are shaped, the eyes move together.

We celebrate in the wake of a new idiom, pilot a rare earth gene magnet
to rise above the pole as my face and her face rise within our unborn
like sap in bas relief that carries a surface impression, lithe imprint
supported from below with our wordless raw character.
Critical aspects that held us and grew us are filtered away
in triage from this fresh wound that prepares for an onslaught
of spring so far in advance that it can't know how to
open its eyes wide enough in darkness to find its way into the world.

So much more than the sum of our parts.
So much more than winter's march abated by spring
but a new beginning that marries our loss with
what we can only hope will be gained
on some level or plane where new things are judged
before they think or act and put something sour into their
toothless mouth that slowly forms a square grimace
before mother earth wrests weak flesh from its comfort
and ease and sets the path before us
before the past imprints and future projections complicate
the initiative, the spark, the cauterization of our deepest heart
to stem further losses of identity and dissolve the illusion
of separateness.

So much more than the love that started it all
and so very much less than the love that will and must
see it through.

Glasses

My first real pair now
forty-seven and blurry from
life's exact price upon me.
A resolution that brings out
the bark in trees, the fine lines
on your face that speak to me;
the real face that I am
bespectacled
looking out for a sign
around the bend on
unlit Rt. 208
to swerve the lit-up
hillbilly on his tractor.

Right to read the riot act to
racy IT techs with dark eyes.
The inflammation is ogling bulge;
mammoth orange spools of cable
roll down the sculptured carpet
to a crashed server.
I am first to get the serial number
off that completely inaccessible tag.
Skew of colors and metal sheen
merges into origin; a bright, cold morning
on a sled, the way my mother called me in
for London broil; my brothers and I
vie to design the best Tater Tot launcher.
I aimed for Lee's horn rims —

A nearsighted visionary can't see his own
reflection clearly, a road sign, a posted notice.
Resumé won't ask, won't tell that I wear glasses now
and might mistake you for someone
I once knew from a place I once
rode my bike through.
So much clearer in the distance
an Adirondack forest awash
in a patina of sun is the show
and I can see
every single leaf.

What I was missing hones regret
the sharp descending serif
the whiskers on my sleeping cat
the old wound of an old wound;
just how terribly we've messed things up
now so much clearer
lens cutting through milky haze of Palisades
at dawn.

Rockface template a passion that chases
the mild curve of glass passing
exits in reflections free of glare.
Years passing without circumstance
until slowly you realize something's changed;
the butter has melted into a
warm golden pool
nooks and crannys balloon affection
crickets dancing on the moon
and then suddenly gone.

A gypsy moth on the window;
the matrix of a foam
lifts the focus to what is real
and what is changing only
because I see it differently
with and without the shift.
Stereoscopic madness dizzy
grasping ghost fabric of air —
Ruddy pores bloom and pearl;
spider gauze rips and drifts down
onto the crumbling deck
driftwood gray
like all four of my eyes.

Blinded by surprise at each rude awakening
caught in the glare of oncoming disappointment
bouncing super-ball google-eyed over wet pavement following thighs.
Audit the sunrise through slits reflecting thruway dashes;
inside lens smeared by unusually long lashes batting sunscreen.
Dialated to the point of vampire cringe forearm shield
inflamed red before raging deadline LCD thumbclick sore neck.
The tech sickness I bought was paid for by loss of focus.
Scope creep hard to wrangle without a wrinkled brow attack.

Will to power brings the fractured image together.
Smoke golden sparkle of crisped leaf
injects the dream overlay; red iris pulse
thunder shakes my skull at the peak —

Cinnamon gold revealed to me in maple going yellow —
Sweet *mutsu* crisp with a scoop of vanilla
in new woodstove crackle firelight.

Shoppin' List

Fort Knox has no gold like Shop Rite;
the sun only mimics itself in victual convection.
All the ore stays rock-locked in the tin mine on aisle 15.
You crawl through the coke display adit — Red sales tag illustrates
what union you link to to dig out a nugget "you dig?"
        Slice big advertising pie on your family budget.

Chain of hysterical laughter echoes over the subliminal public address.
Rather stoned watching MTV on Orwellian viewing screen.
Ain't got no party — Ain't got no alternative disco — Ain't got no foolin' around.
Funny name some bands have like Toad the Wet Sprocket, Hootie and the Blowfish
Big Head Todd and the Monsters, Cracker or
unknowns like Gossamer Albatross and River Run.
I'll call mine Oro Allegro, Sweet Bad Cat, or Fast Gold at Advertising High.
        All this strange karma not on my list —
I am no rock star, not at all but
you never know
what fair balance
is being subscripted to you;
what old dues are makin' new blues for you to croon.

Black and white and red and blue, your shiner
your numb fish
wrapped in wax paper and Saran
just sits there
frozen and lonely.

Who is not where they are? Who's not there in one way mirrors?
Whose-trot-is-even-hotter-in-this-bright-hell!!
        Who-not-in-the-rare-sense-of-the weird!?
Who's-not-in-their-right-mind-choosing-wartermelon?
        Who-balling-freezer-railings-to-reach-something-ancient?
Couldyounotstareblankandinarrears?
Couldyounotstareblanklyatmyrear?
Havin a big ol' time in beautiful Samsara Uptown Market —
Wishinyouwerehere at odds in contrapuntal wackout muzak.
Wishinyouwerenot here — NotwhereItieatwisttie.
Wishing I could eat less; sampling cheezes from a woman mounted on her display.
Aproned, salted and breaded like Betty Crocker in thigh high leather stilletos
serving cold salmon from sterling salver on silverrim china plate with
orzo and dill butter.

"Here have some more of this
delicious golden scarywordsalad sir
with EXTRA etymologousplasticlogoPEPPER!"

II

Sparring from the elbows;
hunched over with sweating fists
to knockout what you call palatable writing
a T.K.O. unanimous anima-decision.

Can't see the cardboard forest for the trees.
Chasing wrapped salmon uptheriverto thesea.
Banging carts with waterontheknee hobbling sadomasobasketball
on a sprained anklet or rather angstlet to exercise some of this
obsessive-compulsive weight off my reincarnated ankhlet
gathering natures in the inner bout of the century!

This week's cover celebrity barfs their hairball
on you as you pass with your radiant cart
full of distilled water and cat litter.
This is the type of thing that you cannot imagine
without a store of back issues of Time and Newsweek so that
all of recent history could join you for dinner.
Bloody steaks and sharp toothed bream wrapped in the latest war pictures;
scales of public figures everywhere
weighing heavy to the question
Is tabloid cannibalism dead? Can we eat it now?
We are lost without our gossip and paranoias
        "Gimme a quahta pahnd that Enquirer cowflop will ya Tony? SNORT!"
Live by the deli, die by the deli, with a nice side of brain slaw.

How many creatures depend on these aisles of gold, this promised land
of cans and plastic bottles; nothing but artifice and sustenance
pale beef suet and gray Romaine, booze in foil Caribbean sunrise pouches?
        I'm losin it in aisle 5
"Attention shoppers...fresh dromedary carrion hacked and
plutonium orchard sour lemon drops arrived to suit your holy holidays!"
Get real soviet and sop it up off the placemat, tickle our underground black market
maven into a gigglescream as she slips into the grinder with Betty.
"Try locusts in marinade of pickled clove syrup, hardened lima bean paste on soda crackers.
Save big on marshmallowed mistletoes and anisette gravy!"

How many moron bankers, traffic cops, wormy ad agency art directors
oblivious insurance agents, and other losers
will I have to bear this winter or just devour
shrinking in their blinking, bleeping violet unconsciousness?

I am getting for *them*, getting *all* this for *them*, getting
holographic scanned and shrink-wrapped, boxed, bagged
and stacked; reclining on the conveyor to serve myself and
you'd better eat me, EAT ME!
          or tangerine dream me, corrugate and hyper-compartmentalize me.
Suffer the little children come unto my Disney Daniel Boone slave ship
stacked with blenders and towels and carmely carmely corn and skinned polecats.
Grieve for the loss of the sugared Heath bar queen bee.
A Sen Sen for three little maids from school are we
tearing open a Glade Solid to cover the tracks of her Charlie
          perfume driving the baggers wild.
I am lost in my list, keeping my eyes down and counting.
I am lost in my list, trying to design the ultimate 90s dish
          synthroTunaShitakeTeriyaki.
Lost in my list with a Catamount Porter cracked and hand in the pretzels.
Lost in the mushroom aisle and can't suppress the smile.
Lost in this trip that wraps masking tape over yr lips, you drink from straws —
          Can't speak of rice and beans without laughing gas.
          Can't plead with the monger to swing his heavy club on the knife blade
decapitating sea bass.
          Can't satisfy everyone who may come over New Years wearing black from
wrist to ass.
It better get better or I will bomb that goddamn ball before it drops
crack a lobster claw and understand Nietzsche once and for all.
Roe-roe-roe yr smelly fuckin' godless boat in the diesel dankness, on a Triscuit.
Your goddamn ant and unkle on crackers get that yellowish haze of old mayonnaise.
Wretched cold cut slapped on day old rheumatoid club roll.
The wurst is yet to come my liver-lovin friends; you turn up the kerosene hat
push through the swinging door with yr breadstick purple and high
to find out what really goes on behind the egg cooler.
          I am lost in my list, havin' a gila monster on rye.
          I am lost in my list, waterin' gums jabbba-jabberin in surprise
as the crusty, grungy housewives slide by on Velveeta slippers
while motorbike lip gloss donut-frost-banged leather eyelash twennybopsters
          frig their littlemiss "I'm so lost in this small town" clitori.
          Their small-change goggle-tongued frat house boot-lickers get even smaller
carryin' multiple 12-packs of Bud shoulder-to-shoulder.

I am lost in a jungle of broomhandles and aluminum.
Goin' around in circles with the Energizer carousel.
Crackin' under the simian pressure of
monolithic bulk rate family sized pickle relish hamster pellets.
Almost ready to glom it all down on this December roadway
and do a Jackson Pollack in the snow;
        recite the Enquirer aloud like gospel to the gathering droves
        caroling the psalm of the
        sharpened incisor.

The Ancients

They carried through the changes, so that the people did what was required of them without being wearied.

When a series of changes has run all its course, another change ensues.

They hollowed out trees to form canoes; they cut others long and thin to make oars.

They used oxen in carts and yoked horses to chariots, thus providing for the carriage of what was heavy, and for distant journeys, thereby benefiting all under the sky.

They made the double gates and the warning of the clapper, as a preparation against the approach of marauding visitors.

They cut wood and fashioned it into pestles; they dug in the ground and formed mortars.

They bent wood by means of string, so as to form bows, and sharpened wood so as to make arrows.

They made their homes in caves and in summer dwelt in the open country.

When the ancients buried their dead, they covered the body thickly with wood having laid it in the open country. They raised no mound over it, nor planted trees around, nor had they any fixed period for mourning.

In the highest antiquity, government was carried on successfully by the use of knotted cords to preserve the memory of things.

Thus, what we call the I is a collection of images.
They are styled symbolic as being resemblances.

Stoned and Coming

Mouth lit up by cellphone glow;
hope amnesia at the next outbreak of calls.
Fall of Rome on HDTV, I bite off
as much as I can chew, plunge into
the Caldera and crank up the jets;
bash the goddamn stress from my bones
like shaking out a garden hose on a slippery deck.

Dark pouch collects the mantra of many tastes —
Again and again I swallow the fire and
speak in tongues, lash each abatement with
terrifying wings, prospect through ice with a branch
and woodstove tongs, heat-accurate to a teepee shaped woodpile.
A branch grown down around a rock, holds it like a tusk.
Pinch by pinch a craft is mounded and set aflame
to dream in swirls of oak and grass, lilac and musk.

Your fingertips paralyze me with pleasure.
Lights turn red in the churning water.
Steam envelops frozen branches above;
early buds push forward.
Mountain of glass lit up by sun ray burst
crumbles in strong wind.
Steam and smoke rise into ice crystals
float down as fancy diamonds to land on your cheek
and melt, back arched over waterfall.

Bright white hot moon on the rise.
Locust stand casts long, dark shadows across gray snow
and you, stoned and coming every night
in steam and in smoke; waves of fog
fall like the dress from your shoulders.

Half-moon like a tongue licks the mountain edge
as it rises
and you, from the water
you held and released in flow
know the spasm of the ice flower
as it thaws;
drawn into the whirlpool
of your thigh
and spun.

Art Action

Art action bites the big chin
drools onto fibre board;
a *giclée* mounted in a golden frame;
worried snapshots of museum walls
dripping with some moldy age.

If dreams and fancies slowed within me —
If I stopped and waited for a moment
to think of rivers coursing through mellow piazzas
where I drank wine and bathed in salt water;
hair wire and skin chalk where the brush meets the burlap
in rapids of color.

Acquisitions of palette knife to carve grapes and apples
in a still life under your chin and lips, so hungry for art action;
wary of my hunger, bestial groaning suddenly befitting your money.

After five 3-hour interviews
I got the job
as Creative Director
of your orgasms in oil;
your soft creaking wicker straddled in-between gessos.

Heaven's rainbow appears as I emerge from a tornado
on the NY Thruway without as much as a memory
of the flavor of your chin.
Here you are with me
smelling of turpentine and linseed
in a perfect, cool, dark pine forest
primordial arcade where I really live.

Washed in sweet rain, your motion, your action;
your eyebrows rise higher into stratospheric applause
like Dali's mustache, reaching brush to gods blue canvas
making a single stroke I can taste.

Smiling Thighs

O to lie down between your smiling thighs
your sweet and smiling thighs, your pearly
and freckled thighs, your monumental
and musky thighs; your warbling hips
snapdragon and akimbo, arching to meet
my hunger.

To part your smiling thighs and enter the
promenade of warm delight, stride
deeply through your musical pavillion
awash in salty rain; to engage your
slick foyer and shake out my umbrella.
To serve tea and oranges on your cinnamon
lawn; to gorge myself in your orchard
be sated by your garden plate, unfurrow
my brow in your wheelbarrow pose
bury my nose in your rose fold.

O to lie down between your smiling thighs
your sweet and smiling thighs, your pearly
and freckled thighs, your monumental
and musky thighs; your warbling hips
snapdragon and akimbo, arching to meet
my hunger.

To sluice your smiling thighs, distill and feather;
drain the robust fruit of its juice cascade down my chin —
To begin and begin again, root and mascerate
those flavors of heaven that prayer cannot elicit.
To meet your wide grin with a temple flame candle lit;
browse in the market where your womanhood sits
urgent and patient and subject to sudden fit.
Roaming blind to find the kind and pouted lips
that caravan my heart in it's straight line trek
to follow the scent of freedom most obediently.

O to lie down between your smiling thighs
your sweet and smiling thighs, your pearly
and freckled thighs; your monumental
and musky thighs, your warbling hips

snapdragon and akimbo, arching to meet
my hunger.

Next Life

Next life I want to call the shots
loud and clear — No suffering.
I don't want any fucking suffering;
I want only fucking and NO SUFFERING.

Next life I want the blinds to be closed;
I don't want to know so much
feel like Moses so much
on the edge of the Singularity
with half a nano-clue;
on the crest of the knee curve
with no view of the promised land.

Next life I want to be there
or I don't want the "gift" at all —
Don't fuck with me on this.

Next life I will cast no shadows.
Next life I will forfeit the grand prize buffalo hide.
Next life I will trust only cats.

Next life I will need no hard drives.
Here's 10 to the 78th cps on a pocket flash drive;
an entire identity ready for re-deployment.
All the thinking of all humans from
the beginning of time is but a single flicker
of that candle.
Next life a million suns will burn in my sky.

Next life I will rise above.
Next life won't be like boot camp.
Mourning doves rebuild their nests, so will I —
Next life when the smoke is cleared.

Next life I will not be a victim.
I will wear the red wool string for protection.
I will chant the fiery song that wards off ego.

Next life I will still react when you freak out
and I will freak out when you react.
My eyes will still wander but not my heart.

Next life you will be with me and
our love will continue
only we won't remember.

Ramapo 500 – Poconos

It takes effort
to get to Promised Land
on Rt. 901 where breakfasts are good.
Sheepskin booties from Shartlesville in the tour pack
for Jesse Mai.

        — abundant green fields — farms
            colts, chickens, goats —

I'm changing from Ketchup to Mustard.
I'm changing from Blue Bonnet to Land o' Lakes
unemployed and in recession.
Better the maestro won't know me homeless
but deciding on which camera to buy
and which lens; messin' with me
to get up close to a necklace or an earring
macroview.
        — Sell a mint chapbook from 1987 — Take Exit 18
feet sink in wet sand, water disperses —
Fish and chips on the beach; clips and ships
all fascinating, not so far away.

We have no choice but to choose.
I am changing from fear to hope
sinking in hot wet sand.
Teal waves break the seal on her fear.
I am changing the ocean to tears
and motor oil and mustard relish.
Saturn spins like a knocking washer;
fast cycle bangs against the drum of space.

The 'Chatterbox' packed with Jersey clubs
"Ghost Riders", "The Complimentaries".
50s Doo-wop LPs cover the walls, an old Yamaha cruiser
a legendary '59 drag racer, a yellow 1936 Chevy —
Great onion rings & burgers, sweet fountain coke;
summer milk maids with trays of fries
hustle across the hot asphalt.

My '09 FLTR motor breaking in nicely — a new friend.

Deep Wood Desire

There is a light coating of dew on the oak and cedar logs of my home.

The fresh scent of evergreen, morning blossoms and deer droppings phase through the air as it changes in temperate zone from hot to cold. I roll out of a warm bed and slide against her hair and skin of silk; setting the iron pot full of fresh water on top of the wood stove, I fan last night's weak ember with a piece of yesterday's news.

There is a light in her eyes as they open to the whistling steam, smell of tea, toasting bread, fragrant oils and incense lit for morning zen. The butter drips and pools beside the bread, her tongue slips over mine, exchanging breaths.

All the lights in the studio are on; the palette of oils pool together into a coffee brown. Vermilion dabs surprise the canvas weave; mixed emotions sieve and filter down to a common denominator — There is only ourselves to please.

All the lights in the sky call me out to play among warm breezes and running streams. I strap on leather with buckle and heavy zipper, rev my sweet V-Twin around twisty mountain lake vistas, come to terms with what I know about the road, what is left behind what is distance traveled, where I go and what pleasure there is in arriving.

There is a light on the floor where my breath goes and I follow.

There is a light in my heart where I have always known no hollow chamber, no beating wings, no butterflies. Oil leaks from the crankcase and I am cranky, testing the limits of pain and desire. Bubbling lamb stew almost ready; oozing linseed color running in rivulets of maize and sienna.

Brush licks like my tongue lays down an image on her belly — Sweat pools and is absorbed by rice paper mixed with ink; a rorshach of orgasm.

Running down a mountain path holding my canvas high; wet paint collecting pollen, leaves and insect, grass brushing by, illuminating my strokes.

The time is passing yet we are continually renewed —

There is a light and I am in it.

My Own Infinity

I

From my first feint *brucha* in *shul*, '*elohainu melach haolam…*'
to pseudobulbar laughter and tears in moments of raw freedom
and auspicious ironic coincidence; absurd mallet hammerdown
before god was an issue, before the blues set the rules;
I directly plugged in to that starry dynamo drumbeat
and the ancient alien who picked my strand from his
belt fob of DNA keys to this universe of mortalities
set my forbears down on bright blue earth, on its dark seas
an egg ready to hatch its genesis payload.

I knew that there was way more to it.
I knew I'd catch hell from
someone out there with a misplaced stake in keeping big secrets;
as secret as the total number of stars
as the number of those with planets not too far
and the number of those with water and air.
I stare at the wall for hours and no world appears.
I catch heaven and hell together in my personal infinitude;
a parsec right or left will mean nothing
and not to be rude but god can go fuck himself.

Need strong breath-fire to forge your breast against columns and chain.
No pride but in surrender to the unyielding life test remaining;
to keep the infinite present while we scurry like ants along streets for crumbs
to widen the mind as the world-bind tightens and confines
to sacrifice nothing because nothing is denied
to abominate the criminal hypocrisy of governments that prate and elevate
the monkey-mind to heights of astonishing homicide.

Kalachakra wheel spins like a razor expanding time-space lengthwise
to expose lost-time-embedded memories; ulterior motives buried in traditions
becoming a man at thirteen, resting on Sundays, blessing the bread and wine.
Hypocrisy in reflection is the common affliction —
First, cloned human slaves dig in desert gold mines
then, Master change his minds and floods us out;
change his minds again and allow us a dawn to dusk grind.
How fucking beautiful and grotesque is that?
My rainbow in that flood covenant spans to an empty copper kettle;
a whole world on its knees and wrung for a single metal.

To rise above by your own sails, you need a strong mast
something to take the torque and strain —
Not spineless faith, but no spine can take it past halfway;
no brain can stay suspended so long
let alone cope with awakening
on the way to your own infinity —
What is it anyway, the infinitely large and infinitely small?
All the same and we're already there
but the day is a drug that causes amnesia
and night disguises dreams we can't maintain or remember.

II

Cat stares at fake paper wasp nest decoy waving
in brisk November wind. His tail snaps back and forth.
Prayer flags twist and bind on snapped branches.

Crushed leaves trail demarks another year in mulch strata.
Piles of limbs and twig hair collect in lawn pockets.
Deer sleep in iris bed right off the edge of the deck.

Orion meteor falls aflame through hard air in full moonlight.
The crystalline sea begat a mast and a line to drag itself forward;
a sextant and a compass, a beacon and warning flag for storms.

Red flesh and blood consumes red flesh and blood; all of it is
meat circus, fang and red eye.
The hunter is out of rehab and curses the drug that causes his hunger
for blood and for fur; for life and for family, the fix is in.

Fall leftovers rot and crush; uprooted stump reaches with its root
like a scorpion, arching back toward itself
to push up new locust shoots with the roots that held.

Full moon comes and goes, gets low and ivory.
Wind blew the leaves off the roof so that work order is moot.
Now they collect in the wind's closets on my deck protecting ticks

so they gotta go. I gotta blow them away but they have a way
of setting up shop again just like that 'pecker that
opens up a new hole in my wood siding as soon as I patch one —

His protection from the cold, his pile of limbs surrounded by brush

his bed of leaves, his starry moonlit sky; his one moment of life
beneath this view, this angle of ecliptic, sector of constellation.

There is nothing to do but stare at the sky; we cannot
put the world ahead of its sheath, it is the knife, the blade
that cuts through black space with gleams of blue, white, green, and yellow.

We see white but there are no white stars; we sharpen the world
but it remains dull by comparison, we just look up and stare
afraid that space and all it holds is impotent to penetrate our petty constructs.

Say it once softly *"I will not abide"* and the antidote thickens.
Say again *"I will never return"* and the joke is on you my friend
as you are constantly returning, you are a mask that changes faces

a voice in sour harmony; kilter and wing begin the flight out of sync.
You fall in just to get going somewhere and then
startled onto a new course you get bearings as the games begin.

With no golden ticket karma seal-coat, the road crumbles
as we move across it; pebbles of blacktop roll slowly in strong wind
down my driveway to the drainage trench filled with leaves.

They make their way to the road and down the road
and along many roads among lovers and tyrants;
a thousand destinations naked and clothed.

Small stones in my tires carried thousands of miles from state to state.
Small minds in Walmart from coast to coast late for work and poorly trained;
tiny little mistakes made tens of thousands of times nationwide.

Where's that good old American ingenuity? Roads, bridges, steel and stone
crumble and erode, pour back into rivers and back to oceans
with centuries precision, precise rust, exacting uplift and dissolution.

Why nothing lasts is not the issue; it's why the past assembles and returns
why the music is a rondo by default. The pasture green and mountain gray
the banana leaf and moist foam of seawaves bake in sun's salt-baste.

Ants chew locust bark and simmer in drops of rain; burning sphere slowly cools
in the icy vacuum of space, awaits first water; a sweaty creased cheek
wakes from its first dream to a new bed of stone with jeweled pillows beneath.

Our faces marked by sleep and by the surface of dream rivers that sparkle with
purpose yet purpose is not at issue; only stop to see the ripples better
bake yourself into a pie that everyone remembers the taste of.

Stealing time to write in and out of whirlwinds of days, hot stove and anvil of mind
being struck to peal and resonate; I'd druther to be wrapping tamales
with splif and satin leaf, green chile sauce on everything.

Why write when words can't ever reach infinity or even the outer concourse?
Why reach when the front is ever expanding outward?
What is the teaching being blared from every hale and hollow orb
that spins feverishly and forever, spun in perfect circles of ice, dust and gas?
Can we sing and hold life high in our hands and eyes without ever knowing that
force?

Circles and people aren't ever perfect, they're random ovate or amoebic.
Snap-to-guides and regulate the stroke but you know some things can't be controlled.
Tilt the axis from self-focus to star gaze; frozen night so scary silent, absolute zero
metronome keeps infernal time; tick tick tick the furnace lights, pipes creak
hot water flows to heat my home, this speck not yet turned to salt.
I have not seen my world yet or any world set in its ways
that can strip real meat from bone
to reveal a lens aligned with unknown eyes.

Distant lenses focus on us and wonder
what real or imagined destinies lie beyond this corked bottle; our ship within
afloat on a vast sea of very real waves caught in yellow iris moonbow eye-light.

III
Ship sails, the mast holds, torque and strain another thing again.
It's all about what it takes to keep afloat in an endless ocean.
Blank faces stare from just below the surface and ripple
in hypnotic waves that kiss the tip of moonbeams simple motion;
the park and ride of our universal commute, the blast of wind again.
Ask and it shall be denied; release the question and prepare for
a mountain of replies. It's your face that counts in the missing reflection
your mountain of lies that crumbles over centuries failed intentions

yet this is my own infinity, my endless friction of cheek against bars
that holds me in my dark hallway until no echo remains. Bars that free me to feel
my way along the border of lives I've made; wagon wheels chatter, warp and splay;
spokes fan out like emanations of entities at play in a spinning furnace.
Their scope of rays burns through the full range of DNA from A to Z;

we are transparent, without parental reprimand, irradiated.
Silent at the doorway, totally unwise to the rush of time outside.
Ill at ease, crepe-thin veil pleats opaque ignorance and ingrained skew.
No way to open your eyes wide enough to see through the illusion —
Transmogrified castle on misty shoreline, piano music distant and feint
as the Adirondack pine is from here. I am zipped up in a jumper, let loose in a
department store, sitting before a plate of sliced cucumber and dill with pureed
eggplant, sliced avocado and onion, a Malbec, and two prime shell steaks, sea
scallops in butter and shallot. In one bite and in one breath and in a single gulp
I pride my desire to captivate the loon and jay with my own guttural reply
as I barrel through folded space alone.

It's all about being loved after all and that's all there is to it.
The best we can do is hear "*I Love You*" about a million times
since people die every day that never know it and pray for it and cry.
The box that contains the best of us is illusory at best
so whatever the test we'll survive, or not, our survival is not at issue.
It's about holding something endless in your heart for even a second
that rips you open from root to gullet when you hear your child say it;
that lasts forever in this cloudy lake of both depth and reflection.

Masts break, ships capsize and sink, big winds continue to blow.
Big minds continue to fret and worry the night away with Jim and Jack.
We got baked chicken wings and rice tonight and the rain is still hours away.
Save us some of what you gathered and we'll leave some prey.
Our jaw and brow may thicken but we will never forget what we know.
Our hands may slow and thoughts linger but we will add something to the
hyperglow. The imprint of our song will last as long as our voices can carry
the tune. The burden of vastness, how much left to learn, tasks remaining
to close, remain.

Here spins a world repaired by exploration yet destroyed by discovery;
a world networked by things yet bereft of insight; a world drilled deep and
running dry, a world criminally unwilling to act on its own behalf, split in
two by blind ignorance. World drips bloodbaths that shrug off the mantle
our blood demands.

Deaf to its inner voices, driven by consumer marketing we stand frozen in time.
Each and every one must crack and bleed in order to move.We must do all and
surrender the shipwheel. Dash and burn like suns vaporize oceans to carry the
salted seed to sky and galaxy. Garden sprouts in a far distant corner of Orion
that looks familiar but not really.

My own infinity from within a spiral of mirrors and stairwells
in this asylum that slowly pulls me from observer to patient
and takes my words away, leaves me bereft, betrayed and silent
with an empty glass at New Years; nothing left but everything
lost at sea with only the wide open ahead and behind, a light snow falling.
Make a wish and send it out on its journey to the end; send it out
without any eggshells to tread and without a hat and shades, a naked wish
that serenades the stars it passes to claim my right to passage.

Unfinished

The philosopher is not exempt from
being selfish because he thinks about
his selfishness
and when unbottled he too turns to a bottle
and a pipe.
He is as unfinished
as each and every simple selfish person
on this planet
and he wipes the sweat from his wrinkled brow
with as soft a mop as he can find
to try without success at making something
anything, easy.

So we remain without completion in all things
and postpone the audit, renovation, staining of the deck
until a bursting need clears the way for
a single thing to happen and that leads to the next thing
that must rupture the ennui
and be taken forward
in friction and sweat and calamity.
Soft things torn against the sand and grit
trees fallen, logged, split, and burned.
Sore limbs stretched out in autumn sun
that cannot reach their limit
the season unfinished within them.

About the Author

Steven L. Hirsch was born in New York City in 1960. Raised in the NY area, he graduated high school from the Storm King School in Cornwall-on-Hudson, NY, in 1977 and earned his B.A. from Bard College in Drama/Dance in 1985. Steve also earned an A.A. certificate degree in Theatre from Naropa University in 1982 where he was a student of both poetry as well as performance arts inspired by Buddhist practices. He was an apprentice to Allen Ginsberg in 1979-1980 at the Jack Kerouac School of Disembodied Poetics and he studied Vajrayana Buddhism with Chogyam Trungpa Rinpoche as well as many other visiting lamas and spiritual teachers.

In 1983, after his junior year at Bard, Steve's father Louis died. He left school to manage his family business of manufacturing bridal veils and accessories in New York's garment center. Concurrently, Steve founded the literary magazine *Heaven Bone* in 1985 to showcase surreal, experimental, and spiritual poetry as well as art, photography, fiction and essays. Along with five poetry chapbooks, an anthology of anti-Iraq War poetry and a collection of fiction, he published twelve issues of the magazine, with the final issue having been released in 2000. Steve finished his B.A. degree credits at the New School for Social Research in NYC while running the family business. Leaving the business to his mom in 1990, Steve entered the computer consulting world and mastered the technologies for digital publishing and marketing workflow management. He is a certified expert in Adobe Workfront and has provided his creative and technical expertise to dozens of Fortune 500 companies for more than three decades.

In recent years he has been riding his Harley all over the Northeast, studying Buddhism and writing, and playing Latin and African hand drums as a founding member of the drum circle "Spirithawk." Steve is the author of *Ramapo 500 Affirmations* (Flower Thief, 1998) and he has had poems appear in *Hunger, Napalm Health Spa Report, Pudding, Big Scream, Hazmat Review, Muse Apprentice Guild,* and *Etcetera* among others.

Steve has performed his poetry at numerous venues including the Core Gallery in New Paltz; the Catskill Mt. Foundation in Hunter, NY; Monkey Joe's Cafe in Kingston, NY; the Dactyl Foundation Gallery, NYC; The Bowery Poetry Club, NYC; A Gathering of the Tribes, NYC; The Howland Cultural Center, Beacon, NY., Colony Cafe, Woodstock, NY, and Penny Lane, Boulder, CO.

Steve resides on Woodcock Mountain in the Hudson Valley region of NY State with his wife Karen, daughter Jesse Mai Lotus, and three cats.

www.ingramcontent.com/pod-product-compliance
Lightning Source LLC
LaVergne TN
LVHW081317110826
845149LV00006B/1531
* 9 7 8 1 9 5 8 2 6 6 0 3 8 *